THE WORKS OF ANATOLE FRANCE
IN AN ENGLISH TRANSLATION
EDITED BY FREDERIC CHAPMAN

MY FRIEND'S BOOK

A TRANSLATION BY
J. LEWIS MAY

WILDSIDE PRESS

MY FRIEND'S BOOK

CONTENTS

THE BOOK OF PIERRE

THE BOOK OF SUZANNE

SUZANNE

SUZANNE'S FRIENDS

SUZANNE'S LIBRARY

THE BOOK OF PIERRE

31st December 188–.

Nel mezzo del cammin di nostra vita
In the midway of this our mortal life

HIS line, wherewith Dante begins the first canto of his *Divina Commedia*, steals into my thoughts to-night, possibly for the hundredth time. But never until to-night has it really touched my heart.

Yet now how intently I ponder it in my mind; how gravely beautiful it seems; how full of meaning. The reason is that now for the first time I can apply its meaning to myself. I, too, have reached the point where Dante stood when the old sun set upon the first year of the fourteenth century. I, too, am in the middle of life's journey —if, indeed, that journey were the same for all, and if for all old age were its goal.

Ah me! I knew twenty years since that it would come to this. I knew it, yes, but I did not realise it. In those days I recked as little about the way of life as about the way to Chicago. But now that I have mounted the hill and, gazing backward, survey at a glance all the distance that I have traversed so swiftly, the verse of the Florentine poet fills me so deeply with the spirit of reverie that I would fain sit through the night here at my fireside calling up the spirits of the past. Alas! how light is the slumber of the dead!

Sweet it is to summon up remembrance of things past. Darkness and silence lend their aid to the task. Night with its calm stills the fears of the ghosts, who are timid and shy by nature, and wait for the hours of darkness and solitude ere they come to whisper their secrets in the ears of the living whom they love.

The casement blinds are drawn close, the door curtains hang in heavy folds upon the floor. One door, and one only, stands ajar, and my eyes turn as though instinctively towards it. Through it there steals an opalescent gleam, and the sound of gentle rhythmic breathing—and not even I can tell which is the mother's, which the children's.

Sleep, my beloved ones, sleep!

Nel mezzo del cammin di nostra vita

As I sit dreaming beside my dying fire, it seems to me as though this house, this room lit by the tremulous gleam of a night-lamp, the room whence comes the soft sound of that innocent breathing, were but a lonely hostelry upon a highway, whereof half already lies behind me.

Sleep, my beloved ones; for to-morrow we set forth upon the road once more.

To-morrow! Time was when the word awakened within me dreams of all that was fairest and most wonderful. As it fell from my lips, strange and lovely shapes seemed to beckon me onwards, whispering softly, "Come!" Ah! how sweet was life in those days. I had confidence in life, the joyous confidence of a young man in love. Not once did I think that, pitiless though she be, she would ever come to deal harshly with me.

I bring no charge against life. She has not wrought me those ills that so many have suffered at her hands. Occasionally it has chanced that, aloof and mighty as she is, she has even suffered me to feel the touch of her caress. In return for what she has wrested or withheld from me, she has bestowed upon me treasures beside which all that I ever longed for were but dust and ashes. But, spite of all, my hopes are fled, and now I cannot hear the word "to-morrow" without a feeling of sadness and misgiving.

No! I have lost faith in life. But yet I am still in love with her. So long as I behold her ray divine shining on three bright, beloved brows, so long shall I say that life is fair, and call down benisons upon her.

Times there are when all seems strange to me, when even the most everyday things thrill me as with a sense of mystery. And so it is that now memory is to me a wondrous thing, and the power to summon up the past just as strange a gift, and a far better, than the power of reading the future.

It is sweet to contemplate the past. The night is calm. I have gathered together the embers on the hearth, and kindled the blaze anew.

Sleep, my beloved ones, sleep. I am writing the memories of my childhood's days, and I am writing them

FOR YOU THREE.

EARLY PROWESS

I

THE MONSTERS

PEOPLE who aver that they can recall nothing of their childhood's days have always greatly surprised me. For my own part I have retained vivid recollections of the time when I was quite a little boy. True, they are but isolated pictures, but for that very reason they stand out in bolder relief from the vague, mysterious background which surrounds them. Though I am still far enough from being an old man, these memories which I love seem to me to proceed from a past that is infinitely remote. In those days the world was radiant with its early glories and apparelled with the hues of dawn. Were I a savage I should take the world to be just as young—or just as old, if you will—as I myself. But a savage, unhappily, I am not. Many are the books I have read concerning the antiquity of the earth and the origin of species, and sadly I compare the transitory life of the individual with the long endurance of the race. And so I know that it is not so very long

17   B

ago that I used to sleep in a cot in a large room
in a big, dilapidated house—since pulled down to
make room for the new buildings of the *Ecole des
Beaux Arts.* It was here that my father lived, a
humble practitioner of medicine and an ardent
collector of the curiosities of Nature. Who asserts
that children have no memory? I can see that
room now with its green-sprigged wall-paper and a
pretty coloured-print which, as I discovered later,
represented Paul bearing Virginia in his arms across
the ford of the Black River. In this room the
most extraordinary adventures befel me.

As I have said, I had a little cot, which stood,
in the daytime, in a corner. At night my mother
used to move it into the middle of the room in
order, no doubt, that it might be nearer her own
bed, the great curtains of which filled me with awe
and admiration. Putting me to bed was quite a
performance. Entreaties, tears, and kisses, all had
to be gone through. Nor was this the whole of
the matter. When I had everything off but my
shirt, I would dart away, leaping hither and thither
like a young rabbit, till at length my mother would
catch hold of me beneath a piece of furniture and
lay me in my cot. It was fine fun!

But no sooner had I lain down than the strangest
individuals, people whom my family knew nothing
about, began to move in procession all about me.

They had noses like storks' bills, bristling moustaches, protuberant bellies, and legs like chanticleer's. They came in one after another showing
themselves in profile, each with one goggle eye in
the middle of his cheek, bearing brooms, skewers,
guitars, squirts, and other instruments that I knew
not. Such ugly beings had no business to show
themselves; but this at least I must record in their
favour: they swept noiselessly along the wall, and
not one of them—not even the littlest, and the
last, who had a pair of bellows sticking out behind
him—ever so much as took a step towards my
bed. It was clear that some power held them to
the walls across which they glided—seemingly unsubstantial things. This reassured me a little, but
I never went to sleep. You can imagine one would
not care to close one's eyes in such company as
that, and I kept mine wide open. And yet, here
is another marvel! I would suddenly find the
room was flooded with sunlight, and no one in it
but my mother in her pink dressing-gown, and I
could not for the life of me imagine how the night
and the weird folk had vanished.

"What a boy you are to sleep," my mother would
say with a laugh; and a fine sleeper I must indeed
have been.

Yesterday, as I was taking a stroll along by the
quays, I happened to see in a picture-shop one of

those books of grotesques, now much sought after, which Callot of Lorraine wrought with his firm and delicate needle. When I was a child, Mère Mignot, our neighbour, who plied the trade of print-seller, covered a whole wall with them, and I used to gaze at them every day when I went out for my walk, and when I came in. I feasted my eyes upon these goblin shapes, and as I lay in my little bed I used to see them all again, and had not the sense to recognise them. O Jacques Callot, what wonders you could work!

The little *cahier* over whose leaves I lingered, brought back a whole world that had faded from my memory. It seemed as though in the chambers of my soul there floated a perfumed dust, and that in its midst there passed the shadowy forms of those whom I had loved.

II

THE LADY IN WHITE

AT the time of which I am speaking, two ladies were living in the same house as we were : one was dressed all in black, the other all in white.

Do not ask me whether they were young ; that would have been outside my range of knowledge. But I know that they exhaled a delicate scent, and that they had all kinds of dainty ways about them. My mother, who was a busy woman, did not care about visiting her neighbours, and seldom went to see them. But I often did, especially at lunch time, because the lady in black used to give me cakes. So I made my calls alone. I used to have to cross the courtyard, and my mother would watch me from her window and tap on the pane when I stood too long lost in contemplation of the coachman grooming his horses. It was a great business to get up the staircase with its iron balusters, and the steep steps had never been made for my small legs. But I was well rewarded for my toil when I got into my ladies' room, for there were countless things which sent me into raptures. Nothing, however, came so high in my esteem as the two porcelain grotesques who sat on the chimney-piece, on either side of the clock. Of their own accord they would wag their heads and put out their tongues. I was told that they came from China, and to China I made up my mind to go. The difficulty was to get my nurse to take me. I was quite certain in my own mind that China was behind the *Arc de Triomphe*, but I never managed to get so far.

Then, too, the ladies had in their room a carpet with flowers on it, and on this I used rapturously to roll. And there was a little sofa, soft and deep, and this became sometimes a boat, sometimes a horse or a carriage. The lady in black was a little stout, I think, and she never used to scold me. The lady in white could be sharp and impatient; but what a pretty laugh she had! We three got on splendidly together, and I had settled it in my own mind that none but I should ever enter the room where the Chinese figures were. I acquainted the lady in white with my decision, and she made not a little fun of me, I thought; but I insisted, and she promised me I should have my way.

She promised me. Nevertheless, one day I found a gentleman seated on my sofa; his feet were on my carpet, and he was chatting to my ladies with quite a self-satisfied air. Nay, more—he gave them a letter, which they handed back to him when they had read it. This annoyed me, and I asked for some *eau sucrée*, because I was thirsty, and also because I wanted to draw attention to myself. The desired effect was obtained, and the gentleman turned to look at me.

" A little neighbour of ours," said the lady in black.

" An only child, is he not?" replied the visitor.

" He is," said the lady in white; "but what made you think so?"

" He seems very much spoilt," was the reply. " He is forward and inquisitive, and just now he is staring with all his eyes."

I was indeed! It was in order that I might see him the better. I do not want to flatter myself, but I understood thoroughly well from the conversation that the lady in white had a husband, who was something or other in a distant country, that the visitor had brought a letter from him, that they were much obliged to him for his kindness, and that they were congratulating him on having been appointed a *premier secrétaire*. The whole thing displeased me, and when I took my departure I refused to kiss the lady in white, in order to punish her.

That day at dinner I asked my father to tell me what a *secrétaire* was. My father did not answer, but my mother said it was a small article of furniture used for keeping papers in. Just imagine! They put me to bed, and the goblins with their eyes in the middle of their cheeks began to move round my bed making queerer faces at me than ever.

If you imagine that, when the next day came, I gave a thought to the gentleman whom I had found with the lady in white, you are mistaken. I had forgotten him with the utmost alacrity, and, if he had so willed, he might have been obliterated from my memory for ever. But he had the effrontery to put in a second appearance. I do not know whether it was ten days or ten years after his first visit. I am at present disposed to think it was ten days. It was, I thought, a most astounding thing for him to come and usurp my place in such a manner. This time I submitted him to a careful scrutiny, and decided that he was wholly unpleasing. His hair was very shiny; he had black moustaches and black whiskers, a shaven chin with a dimple in the middle of it, a slim figure, fine clothes, and withal an air of general self-satisfaction. He chatted about the Foreign Office, what was going on at the theatres, the latest fashions and the latest books, and about the various evening parties and dances to which he had been in the vain hope of finding the ladies there. And they actually listened to him! So that was what they called a conversation, was it! That! Why couldn't he talk as the lady in black used to talk to me— about countries where the mountains were made of caramel, and the rivers of lemonade?

After he had gone, the lady in black said he was a charming young man. I remarked that he was old and ugly. The lady in white laughed greatly at this observation, and yet there was nothing to laugh at in it. But, there! She either used to laugh at everything I said, or else she did not take any notice of my talk at all. She had these two faults, the lady in white, to say nothing of a third which used to drive me to despair. She would weep and weep and weep. My mother had told me that grown-up people never wept. Ah! she had never seen what I had seen. She had never seen the lady in white lying in an arm-chair with an open letter in her lap, her head thrown back, and her handkerchief to her eyes. This letter (I would wager, now, that it was an anonymous one) caused her much grief, which was a pity, for she could laugh so merrily. These two visits put it into my head to ask her to marry me. She said that she had a big husband in China, but that she would like a little one on the *Quai Malaquais*.

Thus the matter was settled, and she gave me a cake to clinch it.

But the gentleman with the black whiskers used to come very frequently. One day the lady in white was telling me that she would have some blue fishes sent for me from China, with a line to catch them with, when he was announced and shown into the room. From the way we looked at each other it was clear that there was no love lost between us. The lady in white told him that her aunt (she meant the lady in black) had gone to do some shopping at the "Two Chinamen." But I saw them there on the chimney-piece, and I could not imagine what in the world going out shopping could have to do with them. But things crop up every day that are so hard to understand. The gentleman appeared in no way distressed at the absence of the lady in black, and he told the lady in white that he wanted to speak to her on a matter of importance. Daintily she settled herself in a listening attitude on her sofa. But the gentleman kept looking at me, and appeared ill at ease.

"He is a nice little fellow," said he at length; "but—— "

"He is my little husband," said the lady in white.

"Well," answered the gentleman, "couldn't you send him home to his mother? What I have to tell you is for your ears alone."

She gave in to him.

"Go, dear," said she, "and play in the dining-room, and do not come back till I call you. Go, there's a dear."

I went with a heavy heart. But it was a very interesting place, this dining-room, because it contained a clock adorned with a picture representing a mountain by the seashore, with a church, and blue sky overhead. And when it struck the hour an engine with several carriages behind it came out of a tunnel, and a balloon rose up into the heavens. But when one's heart is sad nothing seems to offer any attraction. Besides, the picture remained motionless. The engine, the ship, and the balloon only started once an hour, and an hour is a long time—at least it was in those days. Fortunately the cook came in to get something from the sideboard, and, seeing how forlorn I was, gave me some sweets, which soothed my wounded feelings. But when the sweets were all gone, misery took hold of me again. Though the picture-clock had not struck, it seemed to me as though hours upon hours were weighing upon my loneliness. Occasionally I heard the gentleman in the next room speaking with energy. He was addressing entreaties to the lady in white, and then he seemed to grow angry with her. It was all very fine, but when would they finish? I flattened my nose against the window-pane. I pulled the horse-hair out of the chairs, made the holes in the wall-paper bigger, dragged off the fringe from the curtains—heaven knows what I did not do. Ennui is a dreadful thing. At last I could remain there no longer. Noiselessly I crept to the door which led into the other room, and stretched up to reach the handle. I knew I was doing something rude and naughty: but even that made me feel a sort of self-importance.

I opened the door and beheld the lady in white standing by the chimney-piece. The gentleman was on his knees at her feet, his arms outstretched as though to catch her. He was redder than a turkey-cock. His eyes were nearly starting from his head. Fancy getting into such a state!

"Enough, sir," the lady in white was saying. Her face had more colour in it than usual, and she was very agitated. "Since you say you love me, stop and do not make me regret . . ."

She seemed as though she feared him, as though her strength was nearly exhausted.

He got up quickly when he saw me, and I really believe that for a moment he had a good mind to throw me out of window. But, instead of scolding me, as I expected, she threw her arms about me and called me her darling.

She carried me to the sofa, and wept long and

softly against my cheek. We were alone. I told her, by way of consolation, that monsieur with the whiskers was a naughty man, and that if she had stayed alone with me as we had arranged she would have had nothing to cry for. All the same, I found grown-up people could behave very oddly sometimes.

We had scarcely recovered ourselves when the lady in black came in with some parcels in her hand.

She asked if any one had been.

"Monsieur Arnould came," said the lady in white composedly; "but he only stayed a minute."

That, I knew perfectly well, was false; but the white lady's good genius, who had doubtless been with me for some moments, placed an invisible finger on my lips.

I saw Monsieur Arnould no more, and my love passages with the lady in white suffered no further interruption. This doubtless accounts for my re-collecting little about them. As recently as yester-day, that is, after more than thirty years, I was still in ignorance of what had become of her.

Last night I went to the Foreign Minister's ball. "Life," says Lord Palmerston, "would be quite tolerable were it not for its pleasures"; and I agree with him. My daily toil does not demand too much either of my strength or my intelligence, and I have

managed to cultivate an interest in it. But official
receptions are too much for me. I knew that I
should be bored and do no good by going to this
ball ; I knew it, yet I went, for it is part of human
nature to think wise things and do ridiculous
ones.

I had barely made my way into the great salon,
when the Ambassador of —— and Madame ——
were announced. The Ambassador, whose delicate
face had a worn expression—by no means exclusively
to be ascribed to his diplomatic labours—I had frequently met before. He is reputed to have been
very wild in his young days, and there are various
stories going the round of the clubs about his ex-
ploits with the fair sex. He was stationed in China
thirty years ago, and his career over there is
particularly rich in the sort of tales that men like
to tell over their coffee when the doors are shut.
His wife, to whom I had never had the honour of
an introduction, appeared to be past fifty. She was
dressed entirely in black. Some magnificent lace
formed an admirable setting to the shadowy
remnants of her former beauty. I was glad to be
introduced to her, for I set the greatest store on
the conversation of women of riper years. We
touched on a hundred and one topics, as the
younger women swept past to the music of the
violins. At last she happened to refer to the days

when she lived in an old house on the *Quai Malaquais*.

" You were the lady in white," I exclaimed.

" I always used to wear white, certainly," was her reply.

" And I, madame, was your little husband."

" What ! So you are the son of the worthy Dr. Nozière ? You used to be very fond of cakes. Do you care about them still ? Well, then, come and have some at our house. Every Saturday we have a little *thé intime*. Really, how small the world is ! "

" And the lady in black ? "

" I am the lady in black now. My poor aunt died the year of the war. She often spoke of you towards the end of her life."

While we were talking, a gentleman with white whiskers and white moustaches approached us and bowed to the Ambassadress with all the stately elegance of an old beau. There was something about the shape of his chin that I seemed to remember quite well.

" Monsieur Arnould," said she ; " an old friend of mine."

III

"I WILL GIVE YOU THIS ROSE"

WE used to live in a large house full of strange things. The walls were adorned with the arms of savage warriors surmounted by skulls and scalps. Pirogues with their paddles were suspended from the ceilings side by side with stuffed alligators. There were glass cases containing birds and birds'-nests, branches of coral, and a host of spiteful, malevolent-looking little skeletons. I never knew what bond my father had entered into with these monstrous creatures, but I know now. He had bound himself to collect them. Most enlightened and unselfish of men, it was his ambition to cram all creation into a cupboard. He did it in the interests of science; this was what he said, and what he believed. But as a matter of fact, he had the collecting mania upon him.

The whole place was stuffed with natural curiosities. The only room which had not suffered a zoological, ethnographical, or teratological invasion was the little drawing-room. There neither serpents' scales, nor turtle shells, nor bones, nor flint arrow-heads, nor tomahawks found a place ; but only roses : the wall-paper was strewn with them. They were roses in bud, little, modest, timid things—all of them dainty, and all alike.

My mother, who was on anything but friendly terms with comparative zoology and craniology, used to pass her days in this room sitting at her work-table, while I, seated on the floor at her feet, would play with a sheep which, though once possessing four feet, had now come down to three, a circumstance which yet did not render it worthy to associate with the two-headed rabbits that figured in my father's teratological collection. I also had a doll that moved its arms and smelled of paint. I must have been gifted with a deal of imagination in those days, for this sheep and this doll played various parts in a multitude of dramas. When anything of a really interesting nature befel the sheep or the doll I used to relate it to my mother. But to no purpose. Grown-up people, it may be observed, never really understand the stories children tell them. My mother was absent-minded. She never listened carefully enough. This was her great defect. But she had a way of looking at me with her great eyes and calling me " little noodle ' that used to set everything to rights.

One day, in the little drawing-room, she put down her work and, picking me up in her arms, pointed to one of the flowers on the wall, saying, "I will give you this rose," and so that there might be no mistake, she made a cross on it with her bodkin.

No present ever made me happier.

IV

THE PRINCES IN THE TOWER

"E looks like a brigand, this little boy of mine, with his hair sticking up in this fashion. Cut it *aux enfants d'Edouard*, Monsieur Valence."

Monsieur Valence, to whom my mother addressed these words, was an old hairdresser, a lame, but dapper little man, the mere sight of whom reminded me of the horrid smell of heated curling-irons. I used to shrink from him not only because his hands were all greasy with pomade, but because he could never cut my hair without letting some of it get down my back. When, therefore, he began to put the white overall on me and to wrap a towel round my neck, I used to make a fuss, and he would say, "But surely you don't want to go about looking like a wild man, as though you had just come off the raft of the *Medusa*?"

Whenever he had the chance he used to relate, in his deep Southern tones, the story of the wreck of the *Medusa*, from which he had only been rescued after enduring the most horrible privations. The raft, the unavailing signals of distress, how they were driven to eat human flesh—he described it all with the easy-going manner of one who knew how to look on the bright side of things, for he was a jovial man, was Monsieur Valence.

He took too long over the business to please me that day, and did my hair in what struck me as being a very strange manner, when I looked at myself in the glass. It was all patted down quite smooth, and combed straight over my forehead nearly on to my eyebrows, and it fell down on to my cheeks like a spaniel's ears.

My mother was enchanted. Valence had done his work perfectly, and, arrayed as I was in my black velvet blouse, all that remained to be done, she said, was to shut me up with my elder brother in the Tower. "Ah! If they dared!" she added, taking me up in her arms with a delicious air of bravado.

And she carried me, hugging me tightly, to the carriage. For we were going to make a call.

I plied her with questions about this elder brother, and about the Tower, which made me feel afraid.

And then my mother—who was gifted with the divine patience and joyous simplicity of those beings whose sole mission in this world is to love—told me in pretty baby-talk how King Edward's two children, who were beautiful and good, were dragged away from their mother and smothered in a dungeon of the Tower of London by their wicked uncle Richard. And she said, too, having apparently obtained the idea from some popular picture of the day, that the Princes' little dog barked to warn them of the murderers' approach.

The story, she concluded, was a very ancient one, but so moving and so beautiful, that people still painted pictures of it and still acted it on the stage, and that when she saw it at the theatre, all the audience had shed tears, and she with them.

I said that anyone must be very wicked to make my mamma weep like that, and all the other people too.

She replied that, on the contrary, such a play could only have been written by a very noble and a very clever man ; but I did not understand her. I knew nothing then of the luxury of tears.

The carriage put us down in the *Ile Saint Louis*, outside an old house that I had not seen before ; and we went up a stone staircase whose worn and broken steps sent a chill to my heart. At the first landing a little dog began yapping. " 'Tis he," thought I, " 'tis the dog of the Princes in the Tower"; and a sudden wild, uncontrollable panic took possession of me. Evidently this was the stairway of the Tower, and I with my hair cut to look like a bonnet, and my velvet blouse, was one of the little Princes. They were going to kill me! I would go no farther, and clung to my mother's dress shrieking, "Take me away, take me away! I don't want to go up the staircase of the Tower."

"Be quiet, then, you little silly. . . . There, there, then, don't be afraid. . . . This child is really too nervous. . . . Pierre, Pierre, my dear boy, do have a little sense."

But, stiff and convulsed with fear, I hung on to her skirt and refused to be comforted. I yelled, I howled, I choked, staring wildly into the shadows which my terror had peopled with a multitude of mysterious figures.

At the sound of my cries a door on the landing opened, and an old gentleman came out in whom, despite my terror, despite the Turkish cap and dressing-gown in which he was arrayed, I recognised my friend Robin, my good Robin who used once a week to bring me shortcakes in the lining of his hat. Yes, it was Robin himself; but I could not imagine how he came to be in the Tower, not knowing that "the Tower" was a house, that the house was old, and that it was natural that this old gentleman should inhabit it.

He stretched out his arms towards us, his snuff-box in his left hand, and between the thumb and forefinger of his right hand a pinch of snuff. It was he !

" Come in, dear lady," said he ; " my wife is better; she will be delighted to see you. But master Pierre, I fancy, is not very easy in his mind. Is he frightened at our little dog ? Come here, Finette "

I was reassured, and said, " You live in an ugly tower, Monsieur Robin ! "

Here my mother gave my arm a pinch to prevent me, as I understood quite well, from asking my friend Robin for a cake, which was exactly what I was about to do.

In Monsieur and Madame Robin's yellow drawing-room I found Finette a great resource. I played with her, still retaining the belief that it was she who had barked at the murderers of the little Princes. This was why I let her have some of the cake which Monsieur Robin gave me. But one soon wearies of doing the same thing, especially when one is little. My thoughts flew hither and thither like birds that flit from branch to branch, and finally came back once more to the Princes in the Tower. Having formed an opinion concerning them, I was anxious to produce it. Catching hold of Monsieur Robin by the sleeve, I said, " I say, Monsieur Robin, if mamma had been in the Tower of London, you know, she wouldn't have let the wicked uncle smother the little Princes beneath their pillows."

I thought Monsieur Robin did not seem to appreciate the full force of my observation, but when we were alone—mamma and I—on the staircase, she gathered me up in her arms and exclaimed, "Oh! you little demon, you, how I love you!"

V

THE BUNCH OF GRAPES

I WAS happy, very happy. I looked upon my father, my mother, and my nurse as so many benevolent giants who had beheld the infancy of the world and who were unchangeable, eternal, and unique in their own kind. I felt quite sure that they could shield me from every ill, and in their company I enjoyed a sense of absolute security. The trust I reposed in my mother knew no bounds; it was infinite, and when I recall that divine, adorable trust, I feel like blowing kisses to the little fellow that was myself; and whoso knows how hard a task it is in this world to retain a sentiment unimpaired will understand the enthusiasm such memories evoke.

I was happy. A thousand things at once familiar and mysterious haunted my imagination ; a thousand things which, though nothing in themselves, were yet part and parcel of my life. My life was quite a tiny thing, but it *was* a life—that is to say, it was the centre of things, the pivot of the world. Smile

not at that statement, or if you smile, smile with
indulgence and ponder on it.   Whatsoever lives, be
it but a little dog, is at the " centre of things " !

It was a happiness to me to see and to hear.   I
never so much as got a glimpse into my mother's
cupboard without experiencing a delicate and
poetical feeling of curiosity.   What was in it, you
ask?   What was in it, *Mon Dieu!*   Why, linen, sachets,
boxes without number.   I now suspect that my
mother had a weakness for boxes.   She had them
in every shape and size, and in prodigious numbers.
And those boxes, which I was forbidden to touch,
afforded me a subject for profound meditation.
My toys, too, used to keep my little head busy ; at
least, the toys I had been promised, and was looking
out for.   Those I possessed had lost their mystery
for me, and therefore their charm.   But the playthings of my dreams—what splendid things were
they !   Another wonderful thing was the number of
shapes and faces one could draw with a pencil or
a pen.   I used to sketch soldiers.   I would make
an oval for the head, and put a shako on the top of
it.   Only after prolonged observation did I learn to
put the head into the shako as far as the eyebrows.
I was very much alive to the beauty of flowers and
scents, and to the delicacies of the table, and to nice
clothes.   My feathered cap and striped stockings
were objects of not a little pride.   But what I loved

more than any one thing in particular, was the
ensemble of things : the house, the air, the light,
and so on ; life, in a word ! A great sense of well-
being encompassed me. Never did little bird rub
himself with more delicious satisfaction against the
down which lined his nest.

I was happy, yes, very happy. Nevertheless
there was another child whose lot I used to envy.
He was called Alphonse. I never knew him by any
other name, and quite possibly he had none. His
mother was a washerwoman, and went out to work.
All day long Alphonse trudged about the courtyard
or on the quay, and from my window I used to
gaze at him going about with his smutty face,
yellow mop, and seatless breeches, trailing his sabots
in the gutter. I, too, would have given much to
be free to go paddling in the gutters. Alphonse
hung about after the cooks, from whom he received
plenty of cuffs, and now and then a few pieces of
stale pie-crust. Sometimes a groom would send
him to the pump for a bucketful of water, and he
would come back carrying it, very red in the face
and his tongue hanging out of his mouth. I used
to envy him. He had none of La Fontaine's fables
to learn as I had. He was never afraid of being
scolded for getting spots on his blouse ; he was
never called upon to say "Bonjour, Monsieur;
bonjour, Madame," to people concerning whose

doings he was utterly indifferent; and, if he did not possess a Noah's Ark or a clockwork horse, he could play to his heart's content with the sparrows which he trapped, and the street dogs, wanderers like himself; and he could even amuse himself with the horses in the stables until the coachman evicted him at the end of his broom. He was free and he was bold. From the courtyard, which was his domain, he used to gaze up at me sitting at my window as one looks at a bird in a cage.

There was always plenty of life in the courtyard, owing to the animals of every description which haunted it, and the servants who were continually going to and fro. It was a spacious place. The main building which enclosed it on the south was covered with a gnarled and starved-looking old vine, above which was a sundial whose figures had been nearly obliterated by sun and rain, and this shadowy point which stole imperceptibly across the stone surface used to fill me with wonder. Of all the phantoms which I can summon up, Parisians of to-day would find the ghost of this old courtyard the most remarkable. Nowadays a courtyard is about four yards square, and at the top of it, five flights up, you can see a piece of sky about as big as a handkerchief. That is progress, but it is not healthy.

It chanced one day that this busy courtyard,

where women used to come to fill their pitchers of
a morning at the pump, and where the cooks came
about six o'clock to rid their salads of moisture by
shaking them in wire baskets, and to pass the time
of day with the stablemen—it happened, I say, that
this courtyard had to have the pavement taken up;
but they were only taking it up to put it down
again.   As it had been raining during the opera-
tions it was very muddy, and Alphonse, who lived
in the place like a Satyr in his wood, was, from
head to foot, the colour of the ground.   He was
moving about the paving-stones with joyous ardour.
At length, raising his head, and seeing me in my
prison above, he signed to me to come down.
Now, I wanted to play with him at shifting the
paving-stones, very badly indeed.   There were no
paving-stones in my room to be carried about.   It
chanced that our front door was open.   I went
down into the court.

"Here I am," said I to Alphonse.

"Pick up that stone," said he.

He had a savage, unkempt appearance, and his
voice was rough.   I did as I was bid.   Suddenly
the stone was snatched from my hands, and I felt
myself lifted bodily from the ground.   My nurse
was carrying me off in indignation.   She gave me
a thorough good scrubbing, and told me I ought
to be ashamed of myself to "go playing with a

good-for-nothing little ragamuffin of a street boy."

"Alphonse," added my mother, "Alphonse is a common little boy. It is not his fault, but his misfortune; but children who are properly brought up shouldn't make friends with those that are not."

I was a very intelligent and thoughtful child. I remembered what my mother told me, and her words became associated in my mind, I know not how, with what I learned about naughty children in my old illustrated Bible. But my feelings for Alphonse underwent a sudden change. I envied him no longer; no. He inspired me with feelings of mingled pity and terror. "It is not his fault, it is his misfortune." These words of my mother's made me feel unhappy about him. It was well, *maman*, that you spoke to me thus; well that you revealed to me, when I was yet a little child, the innocence of the wretched. Your words were good. Me it behoved to keep them before me in after years.

Well, this time at all events, they had their effect, and I grew sorrowful over the lot of that naughty little boy. One day down in the court he was teasing a parrot that belonged to one of the tenants, an old lady, and I looked down on this strong and sullen Cain with all the compunction of a good little Abel. Alas! that it should need prosperity to make Abels of us.   I cast about for a means of showing my pity.   I thought of sending him a kiss.   But his face was dirty, and my heart brooked not that I should bestow this gift.   I thought for a long time what I could give him : I was in a great dilemma.   To give him my clock-work horse, which now lacked both tail and mane, seemed to me to be going too far.   Moreover, can one convey one's sympathy by making a present of a horse ?   Something suitable for an outcast must be found.   What about a flower, thought I ?   There were some bunches in the drawing-room.   But a flower, that was the same sort of thing as a kiss.   I doubted whether Alphonse cared about flowers.   In great perplexity I looked all round the dining-room.   Suddenly I clapped my hands with delight.   The difficulty was solved.

In a dish on the sideboard lay some magnificent grapes.   I got up on a chair and took a long and heavy bunch which filled three-quarters of the dish. The grapes were pale green, with a golden tinge on one side, and they looked as though they would melt deliciously in the mouth.   But I forbore to eat any.   I ran to get a ball of twine from my mother's work-table.   I had been told not to take anything from that table, but rules are made to be broken.   I attached the grapes to one end of the twine, and then, leaning out of the window, I called to Alphonse and slowly let them down into the courtyard. The better to see what he was about, the boy shook aside the yellow hair from his eyes, and, as soon as the grapes were within his reach, he snatched them, twine and all, out of my hand. Then, looking up at me, he put out his tongue, made a long nose, and departed, displaying his posterior as he went. My little companions had not accustomed me to such manners. At first I felt highly incensed, but reflection restored my equanimity. "I was quite right," thought I, "not to send him a flower or a kiss." This consideration dissipated all my bitterness, so true it is that when one's *amour propre* is satisfied the rest matters little.

When, however, I reflected that I should have to recount the adventure to my mother, I became greatly depressed; but I need not have done, for, though my mother scolded me, she was not angry: I saw it by the laughter in her eyes.

"We should give away what belongs to ourselves, not what belongs to others," she said; "and we should learn how to give."

"It is the secret of happiness," added my father, "and few possess it."

But *he* did!

VI

MARCELLE OF THE GOLDEN EYES

I WAS five years old, and I had formed ideas about the world which I have since been compelled to modify. It is a pity, for they were charming. One day, when I was busy drawing, my mother called me, never reflecting that she was disturbing me. Mothers do these thoughtless things.

This time she wanted me to have my best things on. I didn't see the use, but I *did* see the inconvenience of the operation, and I struggled and made ugly faces about it. My behaviour, in short, was insufferable.

"Your godmother will be here directly," said my mother, "and a pretty thing it would be if you weren't dressed."

My godmother! I had never yet seen her; I did not know her in the least. I did not even know that she existed. But I knew perfectly well what godmothers were like. I had read about them in story-books, and seen pictures of them. I knew that a godmother was a fairy.

I suffered them to comb me and wash me to their hearts' content. My thoughts were all centred on my godmother, whom I was dying to see. But, inquisitive as I generally was, I never asked a single question, though I was simply burning with curiosity.

Why didn't I ask, you say? Ah! I dared not, because fairies as I conceived them love silence and mystery; because there is something secret and mysterious in our hearts which even the latest of us to enter the world instinctively and jealously endeavours to preserve inviolate; because, for the child as for the man, there are things that may not be uttered; because, though I knew her not, I loved my godmother.

I shall astonish you I know—though, happily, Truth sometimes exhibits herself in unexpected guise, which is why we are able to put up with her —but my godmother was just as lovely as my imagination had painted her. I knew her as soon as I saw her. She it was for whom I had been waiting. She was indeed my fairy! I gazed on her with ecstasy, but without surprise. This time, for a wonder, Nature had fulfilled a little child's dream of loveliness.

My godmother looked upon me, and her eyes were of gold. She smiled upon me, and I saw that her teeth were no bigger than my own. She spoke to me, and her voice was clear and musical as a well-spring in the woods. She kissed me, and her lips were cool and fragrant. Even now I can feel their touch upon my cheek.

As I gazed upon her I was conscious of a sensation of infinite sweetness, and the meeting, it would seem, was unmixedly happy, for the memory that I have of it is free from all alloy. It has acquired in my mind a sort of luminous simplicity. Standing erect, with open arms and lips apart as though ready to bestow a smile or a kiss—it is ever thus that my godmother appears to me.

She lifted me up, saying, " My treasure, let me see what colour your eyes are."

Then, running her fingers through my curls, she added :

" His hair is fair now, but it will get dark later on." My fairy could read the future ; but she was kind ; she did not tell me all that was to come, for to-day my hair is neither fair nor dark.

Next day she sent me a present that seemed scarcely suited to my tastes. I was wrapt up in my books, my pictures, my glue-pot, my paint-boxes, and all the paraphernalia of a delicate and intelligent small boy, who was innocently instilling into his mind through the medium of his playthings that sensitive appreciation of form and colour that is fraught with such joy and sorrow for its possessors.

The present which my godmother had chosen did not harmonise with these habits of mine. It consisted of a complete gymnastic outfit containing a trapeze, ropes, bars, weights—everything, in short, with which a boy develops his muscles and trains himself to acquire strength and manly grace.

Unluckily, even at this date my life had taken a studious turn. I had a fondness for cutting out figures by lamplight of an evening. I was keenly alive to the beauty of form and symmetry, but whenever I did forsake my usual occupations, a fit of madness as it were, a sort of riot of reaction, would impel me wildly into games without rule or measure—to play at robbers, shipwrecks, firemen, and I know not what. But all this apparatus of iron and varnished wood seemed to me a cold, heavy, soulless sort of affair, until my godmother taught me how to use it and invested it with some of the charm that was her own. She picked up the dumb-bells in great style, and, putting her arms well back, she showed how to develop the chest by passing a bar between the elbows and the back.

One day she took me on her knee and promised me that I should have a ship, a ship with rigging, sails, and guns at the port-holes. My godmother talked like a veritable old salt : topmast, poop, shrouds, foretop-gallant, mizzen — she had it all quite pat. She used to repeat these outlandish words over and over again as though she were in love with the sound of them. Doubtless they brought many things to her mind, for fairies are at home on the waters.

I did not get the ship. Yet never, even when a very little boy, did I need to possess a thing materially in order to enjoy it, and many and many an hour has the fairy's boat beguiled for me. I could see it then; I see it now. It is a toy no more, but a phantom. Silently it floats upon a misty sea, and upon its deck, lo! a woman is standing motionless, her arms drooping listlessly at her side, gazing before her with great, hollow eyes.

I was never to behold my godmother again.

Even then I rightly judged her disposition. I knew that she was made to shower joy and love on those around her, that this was her mission in the world. Alas! I was not at fault; she fulfilled her mission all too well.

It was not till very many years later that I learned some of the details of her life. Marcelle and my mother had known each other at school; but my mother, who was the elder by some years, was too quiet, too restrained, to cultivate any close intimacy with Marcelle, whose attachments were ardently, almost wildly enthusiastic. It happened that Marcelle's most extravagant manifestations of

affection were excited by a merchant's daughter, a
fat, phlegmatic creature of limited capacity, but
rather inclined to be satirical. Marcelle could
never take her eyes off her; an unkind word, an
impatient gesture from her friend, would make
her burst into a flood of tears. She so wearied
the girl with her vows of friendship, her fits of
angry jealousy, and her interminable letters, that
at length the unromantic damsel's patience was
exhausted. She declared she had had enough of
it, and wanted to be left alone.

Poor Marcelle retired so crestfallen and so
desolate that my mother had compassion on her,
and thus, a short time before my mother left the
school, their intimacy began. They promised to
visit each other, and they kept their word.

Marcelle's father was the best and the most
charming of men, with abundance of brains and a
plentiful lack of common sense. He threw up
his post in the navy without any reason whatever,
after he had been twenty years at sea. People
were astounded; but the wonder was that he had
remained in the service so long. His fortune was
mediocre, and his economic theories detestable.

Looking out of window one rainy day he saw
his wife and daughter struggling along in the wet
with their mackintoshes and umbrellas, and it
dawned upon him for the first time that they

had no carriage. The discovery grieved him sorely. So what did he do, but realise his investments forthwith, sell his wife's jewelry, borrow money from his friends, and hurry away to Baden. Having invented a system that was bound to ensure success, he did not hesitate to stake enough to win the wherewithal to buy horses, carriage, and livery. At the end of a week he came home without a penny, but with greater confidence than ever in his system.

However, he still had a little estate down in Brie, and there he started growing pine-apples. After a year of it he had to sell the land to pay for the greenhouses. Then he went in heart and soul for inventing machines, and his wife died without his observing it. He used to send his plans and memoranda to the members of the Government, the Institute, the learned Societies, and everybody in general. The memoranda were occasionally in verse. Nevertheless, he managed to live. How he did it was a marvel. Marcelle, however, took it all as a matter of course, and went off to buy a new hat whenever a few francs came her way.

She was then little more than a child, and my mother could not understand this way of going on at all. She trembled for Marcelle, but she loved her.

"If you only knew," my mother used to say to

me over and over again ; " if you only knew how
charming she was in those days ! "

" Ah ! mother dear," I used to make reply, " I
can readily believe it ! "

However, they quarrelled, and the origin of the
quarrel was a sentimental affair which, though I
must not leave it in the limbo to which we consign the shortcomings of those we love, it is not
permitted me to analyse so thoroughly as another
might. Indeed, whether I would or no, I could
not go into details, for my information on the
matter is of the scantiest. My mother was engaged
at that time to a young medical man, who, marrying
her shortly afterwards, became my father. Marcelle was most attractive ; you have heard that
often enough. Love was the very essence of her
being ; she breathed love, and she awakened it in
others. My father was young ; Marcelle met him,
and they talked to one another . . . it was enough.
My mother married, and she saw Marcelle no
more. But after two years of exile the fair one
with the eyes of gold obtained her pardon, and the
pardon was so full and free that she was invited
to become my godmother. She had been married
in the interval, a circumstance which, I believe,
contributed not a little to the reconciliation. Marcelle simply worshipped her husband, a villainous-
looking little blackamoor who had been knock-

ing about at sea in a trading vessel ever since he
was seven, and who, I strongly suspect, had
dabbled pretty extensively in the slave-trade. He
had some property in Rio de Janeiro, and thither
he departed with my godmother.

"You cannot imagine," my mother often said
to me, "the sort of creature Marcelle's husband
was. He looked like an imp, a monkey—and a
monkey dressed up from head to foot in yellow.
He couldn't speak any language properly, but he
had a smattering of them all. To express his
meaning he would shout, wave his arms about, and
roll his eyes, though it must, in justice, be admitted
that his eyes were splendid. But don't run away,
dear, with the notion that he came from the Indies,"
added my mother; "he was a Frenchman, born
at Brest, and his name was Dupont."

I must mention, by the way, that my mother
used to refer to every place that wasn't in Europe
as "the Indies," a peculiarity which drove my
father, the author of several treatises on comparative ethnography, to desperation.

"Marcelle," continued my mother; "Marcelle
doted on her husband. When they were first
married one always felt *de trop* when one went to
see them. For three or four years she lived happily
enough. I say happily, for we must take into
account that tastes differ. But while she was over

here in France—you don't remember that; you weren't big enough——"

"But I do, *maman*, I remember it perfectly well."

"Well, then, while she was away, her husband, left to his own devices in the Indies, fell into the most dreadful habits. He used to fuddle himself in sailors' taverns with the lowest of the low. At last someone stuck a knife into him. As soon as she heard the news Marcelle took ship for home. She nursed her husband with all the magnificent energy that marked her every action. But he had a hæmorrhage, and died."

"But didn't Marcelle come back to France? Tell me, mother, how it is that I have never seen my godmother again."

My mother displayed some embarrassment as she replied :

"When she was a widow she became acquainted with some naval officers at Rio, who did her a great wrong. We must not think evil of Marcelle, dear. She was a woman apart and she acted differently from other women. But it became difficult to ask her to our house."

"But, mother, I do not think ill of Marcelle; only tell me what became of her."

"A naval lieutenant fell in love with her, which was natural enough; and he compromised her because he wanted to brag of having made such

a fine conquest. I won't tell you his name. He
is now a vice-admiral, and you have frequently
dined with him."

"What! V——, that fat, red-faced creature?
He has some fine after-dinner stories about women,
the old rip!"

"Marcelle was madly in love with him, and
followed him everywhere. You can quite understand that I am not very well up in this part of
the tale. Anyhow, the story had a terrible ending.
They were both of them in America; where, I
cannot exactly say, I am such a poor hand at
remembering names of places. There he grew tired
of her and, making up some sort of excuse or other,
he left her and returned to France. While she
was waiting for him out there, she learned from
a Paris paper that he was going about to theatres
with some actress or other. This was too much
for her patience, and, ill as she was with the fever,
she sailed for France immediately. It was her last
voyage. She died on board the vessel, and your
poor godmother was sewn up in a sheet and cast
into the sea."

Such was my mother's story, and I know no
more. But, whenever the skies are a tender grey,
and the winds are sighing low, my thoughts take
wing to Marcelle, and I say to her:

"Poor soul in torment, poor soul that wanderest

o'er the immemorial ocean that of old lulled the lovesick earth to sleep, O beloved phantom, my godmother and my fairy, receive the blessing of the truest of thy lovers, of him who, alone maybe of all of them, still doth hold thee in his heart! Blessed be thou for the gift which thou didst bestow upon me merely by bending o'er me in my cradle. Blessed be thou for revealing to me when yet a little child the sweet unrest with which Beauty assails the souls of those who would fain lay bare her mystery. Receive the blessing of him whom, as a little child, thou didst gather in thy arms to behold the colour of his eyes. The happiest, nay, the truest of thy friends was he! On him didst thou bestow the rarest of thy gifts, O most generous heart, for, opening thine arms to him, thou madest him free of the illimitable land of dreams!"

VII

NOTE ADDED AT DAWN

UCH are the gleanings of one winter's night, my first sheaf of memories. Shall I scatter them to the winds, to whirl whither they list? Or were it better to gather them up and bear them to the granary? The ghosts, methinks, will find in them a repast to their liking.

That excellent and most erudite of men, Monsieur Littré, would have liked every family to possess its records and its moral history. "Since," says he, "philosophy has taught me to attach great importance to tradition, and to the due preservation of all that belongs to the past, I have many a time regretted that in the Middle Ages it did not occur to people of the bourgeois class to keep a sort of modest register in which to record the principal incidents in the family life—a register to be handed down and added to by each successive generation so long as the family lasted. What a curious interest would have attached to such of these records, however concise their contents, as might

have survived till our day. What ideas, what experiences, now lost for ever, might have been preserved to us by the exercise of a little care."

Well, so far as I am concerned, I intend to carry
out the idea of this wise old scholar. These reminiscences shall be preserved, and they shall form the
beginning of the Nozière family register. Let us
not lightly cast aside anything that belongs to the
past, for only with the Past can we rear the fabric
of the Future.

LATER EXPLOITS

THE HERMITAGE OF THE JARDIN
DES PLANTES

I HAD not yet learned to read. I was still going about in baby knicker-bockers, and I cried when my nurse wiped my nose; but I was consumed with a thirst for glory. Yes, at the very tenderest age I was possessed by a longing to win immediate renown and to live on eternally in the memory of mankind. My mind was exercised as to the best means to compass this end, even as I played with my soldiers on the dining-room table. Had I been able, I would have gone forth to win undying glory on the battle-field. I should have become like one of those generals whom I used to shift hither and thither with my little hands, and to whom I dispensed the fortunes of war on a piece of oil-cloth.

But it was not given me to possess a horse, a uniform, a regiment, and enemies; and all these things are essential to military glory. It therefore occurred to me that I would become a saint. The outfit is less elaborate than that required for a military career, and saints are held in high esteem. My mother was a devout woman, and her piety—gentle and grave like herself—deeply impressed me. She often read me passages from the *Lives of the Saints*. I listened with delight, and my heart was filled with awe and admiration. I thus got to know by what means the chosen of the Lord rendered their lives precious and meritorious. I learned what heavenly fragrance exhales from the roses of martyrdom. But martyrdom was an extreme to which I was not disposed to go; nor did I think of undertaking the work of an apostle or a preacher, for I lacked the opportunity. My sole idea was to live the life of an ascetic. That was a line of conduct that could be pursued with ease and safety, and in order to lose no time in putting my ideas in operation, I refused to eat my breakfast. My mother, who knew nothing of my new vocation, thought I was ill, and looked at me with an anxiety that it pained me to behold. Nevertheless I persevered with my fasting, and then, remembering the example of Saint Simeon Stylites, who spent his life on a pillar, I climbed up on to the kitchen cistern. But it was impossible to live there, for Julie, our cook, promptly dislodged me. Though I had thus been ousted from my cistern, I pursued with undiminished ardour the way of perfection,

and next decided to imitate Saint Nicholas of Patras,
who gave all his riches to the poor. My father's
study window looked out on to the quay, and from it
I proceeded to fling down a dozen coppers or so
which had been presented to me because they were
new and bright. These I followed up with marbles,
humming-tops, whip-top, and eel-skin whip.

"The child is crazy!" exclaimed my father, as
he shut the window.

I felt angry and mortified at hearing this judgment passed upon me. But I remembered that my
father, not being a saint like myself, would not
share with me in the glories of the blessed, a reflection from which I derived great consolation.

The time came for me to go for my walk,
and they put my hat on; but I tore out the
feather after the manner of the blessed Labre who,
when he was given a hat in the last stages of dilapi-
dation, was careful to drag it in the mire before
putting it on his head. My mother, when she
heard what had befallen my treasures and my hat,
shrugged her shoulders and sighed deeply. I was
really worrying her.

All the time I was out I kept my eyes riveted
on the ground, so that no external object should
distract my thoughts, thus conforming to a precept
frequently laid down in the *Lives of the Saints*.

It was on my return from this salutary promenade

that, in order to put the finishing touch upon my
sanctity, I made myself a hair shirt by stuffing the
padding of an old arm-chair down my back.   But
here fresh tribulation awaited me, for Julie came
in and caught me just as I was engaged in thus
imitating the sons of Saint Francis.   Looking only
on the superficial aspect of the matter, without
seeking the hidden motive, she was merely struck
by the fact that I had damaged an arm-chair, and
consequently whipped me in sheer ignorance.

Looking back over the painful incidents of this
day, I came to the conclusion that it was very difficult to be a saint with one's people about one.   I
understood how it was that Saint Anthony and
Saint Jerome had gone forth into the desert among
the lions and the ægypans, and I resolved to withdraw the very next day into a hermitage.   I
selected, as my place of retirement, the maze in the
Jardin des Plantes.   There it was that I made up
my mind to live a life of contemplation, attired,
after the manner of Saint Paul the Hermit, in a
mantle of palm-leaves.

"In this garden," thought I, "there will be roots
which will serve me for food.   There, too, a hut is
to be found on the summit of a mountain.   In
this spot I shall live amid all the beasts of creation.
The lion which with his claws dug the grave of
Saint Mary of Egypt, will doubtless come to seek

me in order that I may perform the last rites over some anchorite of the district. I shall behold, like Saint Anthony, the man with the feet of a goat, and the horse with human head and shoulders. And, peradventure, angels will bear me from the earth amid the chanting of canticles."

My resolve will seem less strange when I explain that, for a long time past, the Jardin des Plantes had been a place hallowed in my eyes, as somewhat resembling the earthly paradise which I used to look at in my old illustrated Bible. My nurse used frequently to take me there, and I was conscious within its precincts of a feeling of holy joy. Even the sky there seemed to be purer and more serene than elsewhere, and in the clouds which drifted past above the aviary of the parrots, the tigers' cage, the bears' den, and the elephant house, I somehow thought I beheld God, with snowy beard and robe of blue, and arm outstretched to bestow His blessing upon me and upon the antelope, the gazelle, the rabbit, and the dove. And when I sat down beneath the cedar of Lebanon I beheld descending upon my head through the branches the rays which shone from the finger-tips of the Almighty. The animals which came and took food from my hands, looking at me the while with great soft eyes, brought back to me all that my mother had taught me about Adam and the days of primeval innocence. The living things that were gathered together there, even as of old they had found a home with n the floating dwelling-place of the Patriarch, were reflected in my eyes all adorned with a childish grace. And nothing marred my paradise. It did not shock me to behold nurse-maids there, and soldiers and cocoa-nut sellers. On the contrary, I felt happy at being near these lowly folk, these little ones—I, who was the least of them all. All seemed kindly and good to me, because, with sovereign simplicity, I invested every-thing with the glamour of my own childish ideal.

I fell asleep fully resolved to go and dwell in this garden, in order that I might become meritorious and achieve equality with the great saints whose elaborate history I remembered.

Next morning my resolution was firm as ever, and I disclosed the matter to my mother. She began to laugh.

"Whoever put it into your head to become a hermit and dwell in the maze of the Jardin des Plantes?" she asked, combing my hair and laughing all the while.

"I want to be a celebrity," said I; "to be able to put on my visiting cards, 'Hermit and Saint of the Calendar,' just as father has 'Laureate of the Academy of Physicians and Secretary of the Anthropological Society' on his."

At this my mother dropped the comb with which she was doing my hair, exclaiming, "Pierre, Pierre, how foolish and, oh! how wicked! Oh! how unfortunate I am! Here, my little boy has lost his wits before most people have any to lose."

Then, turning to my father:

"You heard that?" said she; "he is seven, and he wants to be a celebrity."

"My dear," replied my father, "mark my words, when he is twenty he will have grown sick of fame."

"God grant it may be so!" said my mother; "I do not like vain people."

God did grant it, and my father's words came true. Like the king of Yvetôt, I get on very well without renown, and I have not the smallest wish to inscribe the name of Pierre Nozière in the memory of my fellow-men.

Nevertheless, whenever I come, with my long train of far-off memories, to wander in these gardens, now so lonely and so desolate, I feel unaccountably impelled to seek some friendly stranger and tell how once, long ago, it had been my ambition to become a hermit there; as if my childish tale mingling with the stranger's thoughts could bestow on him the blessing of a smile.

It is also a great question with me whether I really acted wisely in relinquishing, at the age of six, all idea of following a military career. For it is a fact that I have never thought of being a soldier since. This I am a little disposed to regret There is a splendid dignity about the life of a soldier. For him the path of duty is clearly defined, not the less clearly because reason has no part in defining it. The man who seeks out reasons for what he does soon finds out that few of his reasons are blameless. Only a priest or a soldier is untortured by the stings of doubt.

As to becoming a hermit, the plan has recurred to me every time I have felt convinced that life is fundamentally bad. That is to say, every day. But every day Nature has reasserted her sway and reawakened my interest in those doings in which ordinary men and women pass their lives.

II

PÈRE LE BEAU

SOME of the portraits one meets with in Heine's Memoirs, though strikingly realistic, are clothed with an atmosphere of poetry. Such is the picture which the poet draws of his uncle Simon Van Geldern.

"My uncle," says Heine, "was an eccentric old fellow whose external appearance was of the humblest, yet quaintest, description. He was a quiet, unobtrusive little body, with a pale, severe cast of countenance, and his nose, though Grecian in its outline, was at least a third longer than the Greeks themselves were in the habit of wearing those appendages. He invariably went about in clothes of antique cut, and wore the knee-breeches, white silk stockings, buckle shoes, and pigtail of the old *régime*. As the worthy little gentleman trotted with short, mincing footsteps across the street, this pigtail would bob about from shoulder to shoulder, cutting all sorts of capers, as though it were mocking at its proprietor behind his back.

"The little man was possessed of a most magnanimous soul, and beneath his little swallow-tailed surtout there beat the heart of the last survivor of the days of chivalry. But, knight though he was, he was not of the errant order. He never wandered far from his little ancestral home at Düsseldorf—'Noah's Ark,' as it was called, from a cunningly carved and gaudily painted ark that surmounted the doorway. There he was free to indulge uninterruptedly in all his tastes: his little puerilities of scholarship, his book-collecting, and his mania for scribbling—a mania which found an outlet principally in political gazettes and obscure little reviews.

"Ardour for the common weal it was that drove Simon Van Geldern into authorship. He took immense pains over his compositions. Thinking alone, to say nothing of writing, was a desperate effort for him. He wrote in the stiff, pedantic style that he had acquired at the Jesuit schools.

"It was this uncle," Heine tells us, "who exerted a great influence in the formation of my mind, and, on this point, I owe him a debt of infinite gratitude. Widely sundered as were our ideas, his literary aspirations, pathetic though they were, may possibly have helped to awaken in me the ambition to achieve distinction in literature."

This description of the old man Van Geldern

reminds me of another quaint figure whose portrait
—as I have but my own recollections to draw upon
—will, I am afraid, appear but faint and unattractive
in comparison. But I could never hope to sketch a
likeness with that wonderful blend of fidelity and
fantasy which is the distinguishing characteristic of
Rembrandt and Heine. It is unfortunate, for the
original was worthy of a skilful artist.

Yes! I, too, had a Simon Van Geldern to inspire
my childish mind with a taste for things intellectual
and an incorrigible desire to write. He was called
Le Beau, and it is perhaps to him that I owe the
habit—that has been mine since I was fifteen years of
age—of covering unlimited paper with records of my
meditations. I know not whether I ought to thank
him ; but, at all events, the failing with which he inspired me was as harmless and as innocent as his own.
His mania was compiling catalogues. Week in, week
out, he catalogued and catalogued and catalogued.
He excited my admiration, and, when I was ten, I
thought that to make a catalogue was a finer thing
than to win a battle. Since then my ideas have de-
generated somewhat, but in reality my opinions have
not altered so much as one might suppose. Père
Le Beau, as he used to be called, is still, to my mind,
a man to be envied and extolled ; and if I occasionally indulge in a smile, as I think of this old friend
of mine, it is a smile all kindness and affection.

Père Le Beau was very old when I was very young: for which reason there was an excellent understanding between us.

Everything about him inspired me with a trustful curiosity. His spectacles perched on the end of his nose, which was big and round; his plump, ruddy countenance, his flowered waistcoat, his ample dressing-gown with its pockets stuffed full of old books—his whole appearance, in a word, conveyed a suggestion of good-humour that a touch of the motley only served to enhance. He wore a low-crowned hat with wide brims, around which his white hair twined and clustered like honeysuckle about the rail of a garden terrace.

Everything he said was simple, short, and graphic, like a tale for children. He was naturally of a simple disposition, and kept me amused without the slightest effort on his part. Being a great friend of my parents, and regarding me as a quiet and intelligent little boy, he encouraged me to go and see him in his house, where he had scarcely any visitors but the rats.

It was an old house, standing somewhat back from a steep, narrow street which leads to the Jardin des Plantes, a street which in those days, I imagine, harboured all the cork-makers and coopers of Paris. There was an odious smell of wine casks about the place that I shall remember to my dying day. You had first of all to follow Nanon, the old servant, across a little parsonage garden, and then, after ascending some stone steps, you would find yourself in what was assuredly the most extraordinary of dwellings. Mummies, ranged all along the lobby wall, bade you welcome as you entered. One was enclosed in its gilded sheath, others had nothing but blackened linen about their shrivelled bodies, and one in particular, freed from its cerements, displayed its white teeth and enamel eyes. Nor was the staircase less alarming : chains, pillories, prison keys bigger than your arm, hung in profusion on the walls.

Like Bouvard, Père Le Beau would have been quite equal to including a disused gallows in his collection, and, indeed, he did possess Latude's ladder and a dozen or so choke-pears. The four rooms that comprised his dwelling were all alike. Books were piled up right to the ceiling and littered the floors, intermingled in hopeless confusion with maps, medals, armour, flags, smoke-begrimed pictures, old broken bits of carving in wood or stone. Heaped upon a rickety table and a worm-eaten chest stood a mountainous pile of coloured pottery.

Everything that one could possibly hang hung from the ceiling in woeful attitudes. A uniform coating of dust rendered everything in this chaotic

collection more or less indistinguishable, and each
object seemed only to be kept in place by the
countless spiders' webs which surrounded it, for
Père Le Beau, who had his own notions concerning
the preservation of works of art, forbade Nanon to
sweep the floors. A most remarkable thing, however, was that everything had either a forlorn or
leering expression, and looked spitefully at one, as
though the whole place were tenanted by people
metamorphosed and held in thrall by evil spirits.

Père Le Beau was usually to be found in his bedroom, which was in just as great a muddle as the
rest of the house, but not so dusty, for there the
old servant had leave to ply her broom and feather-
brush. Half the space was taken up by a long
table smothered with little pieces of cardboard. At
this table my old friend, attired in his flowered
dressing-gown and night-cap, used to work with all
the joy of a peaceful, unsophisticated soul. He
catalogued, and I looked on in wide-eyed, breathless
admiration. He catalogued books and medals
chiefly, assisting his vision with a magnifying-glass.
He covered his little pieces of cardboard with a
small, regular, and cramped hand. I did not think
that anyone could devote himself to a finer occupation. I was wrong. A printer was found to print
the catalogue of Père Le Beau, and then I beheld
my friend correcting proofs. He made mysterious

marks in the margin of the cards, and then I knew that this was the finest task the world could offer; and I stood agape with wonder and admiration.

After a while I grew more daring, and vowed that I, too, would have proofs to correct one day. The aspiration has not been fulfilled, but it is a circumstance which I regard with qualified regret, for I have discovered from intercourse with a friend of mine—a literary man—that everything becomes irksome after a time, even proof-correcting. Nevertheless it was this old friend that determined the course my life was to take. The unusual spectacle afforded by the contents of his abode accustomed me to the sight of what was old and rare, turned my gaze backwards towards the past. By the example he afforded me of the regular untroubled execution of a piece of literary spade-work, he implanted in me, even as a child, the desire to work for the improvement of my mind. In conclusion, I owe it to him that I have developed into a great reader, a zealous annotator of ancient texts, and that I am here writing these memoirs that will never find their way into print.

I was twelve years old when this kindly but eccentric old man passed peacefully away. His catalogue, as you can well imagine, was never published; and the mummies and the rest of the things were sold by Nanon to the dealers.

Last week I happened to come across one of those little models of the Bastille which Palloy the patriot used to carve out of stones that had belonged to the demolished fortress, models which he offered—for a consideration—to the municipal bodies and the general public. The thing was by no means scarce, and it was very unwieldy. I examined it, however, with instinctive curiosity, and it was not without emotion that I read, on the base of one of the towers, the half-obliterated legend: "From the collection of Monsieur Le Beau."

III

GRANDMAMMA NOZIÈRE

THAT morning my father looked very much upset. My mother was bustling about and speaking in an undertone. In the dining-room a sewing woman was busily employed making black dresses.

Luncheon, too, was a melancholy affair, and the conversation was conducted in whispers. I knew quite well that something had happened.

At length my mother, dressed all in black and thickly veiled, came to me and said, "Come, my dear."

I asked her where we were going, and she said:

"Pierre, listen to me! Your grandmamma Nozière—you know, your father's mother—died last night. We are going to say good-bye to her, and to kiss her for the last time."

And I saw that my mother had been crying. As for the effect on myself, it was very great, for all these years have not availed to obliterate it; but it was also very vague, for I cannot describe it in words. I cannot say that it was a melancholy effect, or if it was, the sadness had nothing terrible in it. My state of mind was caused by nothing external or tangible, and on the whole the most fitting epithet to apply to it is perhaps "romantic."

All the way along, my thoughts were centred upon my grandmother, but I could form no idea of what it was that had befallen her. Death! I could not imagine what that could possibly be. But I knew that the hour of death was a serious one.

By a not altogether inexplicable illusion, I thought as I drew near the house of mourning that the aspect of the immediate surroundings and all the neighbourhood had some connection with my grandmother's death, and that the morning quiet of the streets, the voices of the neighbours, the people hurrying by, the sound of the blacksmith's hammer, were all to be ascribed to the same cause. This idea wholly engrossed me, and with this mysterious thing called "Death" I also associated the beauty of the trees, the radiance of the sky, and the softness of the air.

I felt as though I were treading a path of mystery, and when, at a turn in the road, I beheld the little garden and the cottage that I knew so well, I was almost disappointed at discovering nothing out of the ordinary. The birds were singing.

A sense of fear came over me, and I looked up at my mother. Her eyes were fixed with an expression of religious awe on a spot toward which I in turn directed my gaze.

Then I perceived, glimmering through the white-curtained window of my grandmother's room, a light, a pale, unsteady light. And this light seemed so death-like amid the exceeding brightness of the day, that I bowed my head that I might see it no more.

We went up the little wooden staircase and through the silent rooms. When my mother put out her hand to open the bedroom door, I clutched it as though to hold her back. We went in. A nun, who was sitting in an arm-chair, rose and made room for us at the head of the bed. My grandmother was lying there, and her eyes were closed.

It seemed to me that her head had grown very heavy—heavy as a stone, so deep was the pit it made in the pillow! Her hair was hidden beneath a white cap; she did not look so old as usual, although her face was colourless.

Oh! how little her appearance resembled sleep! But what was the meaning of that little insistent smile that was so painful to behold?

I thought her eyelids trembled a little now and then, doubtless because they were exposed to the flickering light of the two tapers that were burning on the table, one on either side of a bowl of holy water in which a sprig of box was lying.

"Kiss grandmamma," said my mother.

I touched the face with my lips, and the chill that went through me I cannot, nor ever shall be able to, describe.

I covered my eyes, and I heard my mother sobbing.

Really, I do not know what would have become of me had not my grandmother's servant taken me out of the room.

She led me by the hand, and took me to a toy-shop, and said :

"Choose what you like." I chose a cross-bow, and began to amuse myself shooting peas in among the leaves of the trees.

I had forgotten my grandmother. It was only in the evening, when I saw my father, that the thoughts of the morning came back to me again. My poor father was no longer recognisable. His face was all swollen and drawn. His eyes were brimming, and his lips quivering convulsively.

My mother was sitting at his side writing addresses on black-edged paper. Some relatives came in to help her. I was shown how to fold the letters. There were about a dozen of us seated round a large table. It was warm. The task I

had to perform was a new one; this gave me a
feeling of importance and kept me amused.

After her death it seemed that my grandmother
lived again, and that this second life was more
remarkable than the first. I remembered with
incredible vividness everything I had seen her do or
heard her say. And my father used to tell us
stories about her every day that brought her before
us in her habit as she lived; and sometimes at
night, after dinner was done, it almost seemed as
though she had been there breaking bread with us.
Oh! why did we not speak to this dear shade as
the pilgrims of Emmaus spake to the Master?

"Abide with us : for it is toward evening, and
the day is far spent."

Ah! what a sweet ghost she made, with her
lace bonnet and green ribbons. It was difficult—
impossible—to imagine how she would adapt herself to the conditions of the other world; with
nobody was the idea of death so difficult to associate
as with her. Death may come to a monk, or to
some beautiful heroine; but that the cold grave
should claim a laughter-loving, light-hearted,
daintily-attired little old lady, such as grandmamma
Nozière—how impossible it seemed !

I will tell you something I found out all by
myself about her when she was still alive.

Grandmamma was frivolous ; yes, grandmamma's

ideas about morality were not of the strictest; grandmamma had no more piety in her composition than a bird. You ought to have seen the little quizzical grimace she would make on Sundays when mother and I were setting out for church. She used to smile at the seriousness which my mother brought to bear on everything connected with this world and the next. She readily forgave me my faults, and I think she would have forgiven bigger ones than mine.

"He will be a very different sort of fellow from his father," she used to say of me. By that she meant that I should spend my young days dancing, and fall in love with countless maidens. She flattered me. As a matter of fact, the only thing she would approve in me, if she were still of this world (she would be a hundred and ten by this time), would be that I can take life very comfortably, and that I possess a happy tolerance in regard to the views of others—advantages I have purchased, not too dearly as I think, by the sacrifice of a few moral and political shibboleths. These were qualities which, in my grandmother, had all the attractiveness of natural gifts; she died without being aware that she possessed them. My inferiority lies in my *consciousness* of being tolerant and sociable.

My grandmother was real eighteenth century.

There was no doubt about that! I regret that no one ever wrote the story of her life. To do so herself would have been quite out of her line. But why could not my father have undertaken the task instead of measuring the skulls of Papuans and Bosjemans?

Caroline Nozière was born at Versailles on the 16th April 1772. She was a daughter of that Doctor Dussuel, of whose talents and character Cabanis used to speak so eulogistically. Dussuel it was who, in 1789, was called in to attend the Dauphin in a slight attack of scarlatina. One of the Queen's carriages would fetch him daily from Luciennes, where he used to live in comparative poverty, with his books and his herbarium about him, like a true disciple of Jean-Jacques. One day the carriage came back to the palace empty: the doctor had refused to come.

"So you had forgotten us, monsieur," said the Queen in irritated tones, on his next appearance.

"Madame," replied Dussuel, "your reproaches wound me, but they do honour to your natural instincts, and I must forgive them in a mother. Have no misgivings; I am treating your son with every care; but yesterday I was called to attend a peasant woman at her lying-in, and I could not leave her."

In 1789 Dussuel published a brochure which I

cannot open without respect, or read without a smile. It is entitled, *Les Voeux d'un Citoyen;* and for a motto it has the words, *Miseris succurrere disco.* The author begins by referring to the aspirations which he, beneath his humble roof, has formed for the well-being of the French people. He then proceeds to trace, with simple candour, his rules for ensuring the public welfare. They were founded upon a basis of enlightened liberty, a liberty that was to be safeguarded by constitutional guarantees. He concluded by commending to the gratitude of all men of feeling, Louis XVI., monarch of a free people; and he foretold the early return of the Golden Age.

Three years later, his patients—they were also his friends—were having their heads cut off, while he himself, suspected of Moderatism, was taken to Versailles by order of the Committee of Sèvres, and shut up in the Franciscan convent, which had been turned into a prison. There he arrived covered with dust, and looking much more like an aged beggar than one learned in medicine and philosophy. Having deposited a little bag containing the works of Raynal and Rousseau on the floor, he sank back into an arm-chair, exclaiming with a sigh:

"Is this, then, the reward of fifty years of virtue?"

At this point a young woman of great beauty,

whose presence he had not at first observed, came forward with a basin and sponge, saying :

"There is reason, monsieur, to believe that we shall soon be guillotined. Will you, in the meantime, allow me to wash your face and hands, for you have made yourself look like a wild man ? "

"Compassionate being," exclaimed the aged Dussuel; "is it, then, here, within these haunts of crime, that I am fated to encounter you ? Your youth, your countenance, your actions, all alike assure me of your innocence."

"My sole crime," replied the fair captive, "is to have bewailed the death of the worthiest of kings."

"Louis XVI. had his good qualities," replied my great-grandfather ; "but what a pinnacle of fame might he not have attained had he remained truly loyal to this glorious Constitution."

"What! monsieur," exclaimed the young woman, brandishing her dripping sponge, "are you, then, a Jacobin ? Are you, too, on the side of the plunderers ? "

"And you, madame, are you at one with the enemies of France ? " sighed Dussuel, whose ablutions were but half completed. "Can a feeling heart beat in the bosom of an aristocrat ? "

The lady's name was De Laville, and she had gone into mourning for the king. During the four months that she and Dussuel were shut up together, she was always upbraiding him, and always trying to think of some means of making him comfortable. Contrary to their expectation, they were not guillotined. On the strength of a report drawn up by Battelier, the Deputy, they were set at liberty ; and Madame de Laville afterwards became my grandmother's closest friend. My grandmother was then twenty-one years old, and had been married for three years to the citoyen Danger, adjutant-major of a volunteer battalion of the Upper Rhine.

"He is a very good-looking man," my grandmother used to say ; "but I'm not at all sure that I should know him if I met him in the street."

She averred that she had seen him but five times, and that she had not been in his company for more than six hours altogether. She had only married him in a moment of girlish caprice, because she wanted to wear her hair *à la nation*. The truth was, she didn't want a husband at all. He, on the other hand, wanted all the women in the world. Eventually he left her, and she let him go without the least trace of resentment.

When he set out upon the path of glory, the only property with which Danger endowed his wife was contained in one of the pigeon-holes of his secretaire. It consisted of some receipts for money which he had advanced to a brother of his, one

Danger de St. Elme, an officer in Condé's army, and a packet of letters he had received from some *émigrés*—material, in short, that would have abundantly sufficed to bring my grandmother, and fifty people besides, to the guillotine.

Indeed, she herself was not without misgivings about the matter, and every time a domiciliary visit took place in the neighbourhood, she would say to herself, " Really, I *must* burn the papers that rascally husband of mine left behind him." But she always had a hundred different ideas in her head at once. One morning, however, she made up her mind that she would put the thing off no longer.

She had chosen the right moment, and no mistake !

She had taken the papers out of the secretaire and spread them all over the sofa, and she was sitting in front of the fire looking them over, leisurely putting them into little piles, sorting out those which she could keep from those she would have to destroy. She was reading a line here and a line there, gathering up little fragments of the past as she pursued her task, when all of a sudden she heard the door of the house open. Instinctively it flashed upon her that this was a domiciliary visit. Hastily gathering up the scattered papers in one huge armful, she pitched them in under the sofa, the cover of which reached right down to the floor,

giving them a kick to get them well back. Even
as it was, the corner of a letter was sticking out
like the tip of a white cat's ear, when a representative of the Committee of General Surety came
striding into the room, followed by six men of the
section armed with muskets, swords, and pikes.

Madame Danger was standing up in front of the
sofa. She reflected that her undoing was not yet
a matter of absolute certainty ; she deemed that she
had, perhaps, just one chance out of ten thousand,
and she became keenly interested in the course that
the proceedings were about to take.

"Citoyenne," said the president of the section,
"you have been accused of holding treasonable
correspondence with the enemies of the Republic.
We have come to take possession of all your
papers."

The representative of the Committee of General
Surety then sat himself down on the sofa, and
prepared to draw up a report of the seizure.

His men then proceeded to turn the place upside
down. They forced the locks, and turned out the
drawers. Finding nothing there, they broke open
the cupboards, stove in the cabinets, turned the
pictures, and prodded their bayonets into the
arm-chairs and the cushions. They banged on
the walls with the butt-end of their muskets,
looked up the chimneys, and tore up pieces of the

flooring—but all to no purpose. Finally, after three hours' fruitless search and useless destruction, they withdrew in despair, worn out and crestfallen ; but loudly proclaiming their intention of returning to the charge. It had never occurred to them to look under the sofa !

A few days after this, my grandmother was coming home from the theatre, and had just reached her front door, when she was confronted by a half-starved, white-faced creature, with a dirty, grey beard of several days' growth disfiguring his countenance, who cast himself on his knees before her, crying piteously :

"Citoyenne Danger, I am Alcide ; save me, I beseech you, save me ! "

And then she saw who it was.

"Mon Dieu ! " she exclaimed, " is it possible ? Are you really Monsieur Alcide, my dancing-master ? Fancy seeing you again in this plight, Monsieur Alcide."

"There is a price on my head, citoyenne ; save, oh, save me ! "

"I will do what I can. I am a suspect myself, and my cook is a Jacobin. But, come, follow me ! Only take care my porter doesn't see you ; he is a Municipal officer."

Up the stairs they went, and this little trump of a woman locked herself in with the luckless Alcide, who was shaking from head to foot with fever, and kept saying over and over again, his teeth chattering with terror : " Save me ! save me ! "

Pitiable as his condition was, she could scarcely suppress a laugh. But the situation was a critical one.

" Where on earth can I stuff him ? " said my grandmother to herself, as she gave a hurried glance at the cupboards and chests.

For want of a better place, she at last bethought herself of putting him in her own bed.

She drew out two of the mattresses beyond the others so as to form a sort of trough on the side next the wall. Into this trough she bundled Alcide. This gave the bed a very tumbled appearance, so she undressed and got into it. Then she rang for the cook.

" Zoe," said she, " I'm not well. Let me have a chicken, some salad, and a bottle of claret ; and— Zoe !—what is the news to-day ? "

" Why, those ruffians of aristocrats have been at their plots again. They won't be satisfied till they have been guillotined, every man Jack of 'em. But the *sans culottes* have got an eye on 'em. The porter tells me that they are hunting for a black-guard called Alcide in this district, and that you may rely on having a domiciliary visit to-night."

Alcide, between his two mattresses, had been

listening to this gentle discourse, and when Zoe had gone out of the room, he was seized with a fit that fairly shook the bed, and his breathing became so painful that the whole room was filled with a sort of strident wheezing.

"Here's a pretty go!" quoth little Madame Danger to herself.

And she proceeded to devour a wing of the chicken, and passed down a nip or two of wine to the lugubrious Alcide.

"Ah! madame! Ah! Jesus!" cried Alcide; and he began to weep with more noise than discretion.

"Splendid," said Madame Danger to herself; "the Municipal people have only got to put in an appearance and——"

She had reached this point in her reflections, when the rattle of muskets being brought heavily to the ground made the landing shake.

Zoe ushered in four Municipal officers and thirty men belonging to the National Guard.

Alcide did not budge an inch now, and nothing, not so much as a sigh, was heard of him.

"Now then, citoyenne," said one of the Guards, "up you get!"

But one of his comrades pointed out that the citoyenne could not very well dress herself in front of a party of men.

Catching sight of the bottle of wine, one of the fellows picked it up and helped himself; and the others swilled at it with gusto.

One merry wight seated himself on the bed, and, chucking Madame Danger under the chin, exclaimed, "What a pity such a pretty face should belong to an aristocrat; what a shame to cut into this nice little neck."

"Come," said Madame Danger, "I see you're good-hearted fellows. Make haste, look at whatever you have got to look at, for I'm simply dying to get to sleep."

For two mortal hours did they stay in that room. A score of times they must have gone past the bed and looked to see if there was anyone underneath it. But, at last, after delivering themselves of endless gibes and impertinences, they took their departure.

Scarcely was the last man's back turned, when little Madame Danger leaned over the edge of the bed, calling out, "Monsieur Alcide! Monsieur Alcide!"

"Good gracious," a rueful voice replied, "they will hear us! For Christ's sake, have pity on me, madame!"

"Monsieur Alcide," my grandmother went on, "a pretty fright you have given me. I could hear nothing of you. I thought you were dead, and the idea of lying on a dead man nearly sent me into a fit. Monsieur Alcide, you don't play fair. When a person isn't dead, why, gracious me, he should say so. I shall never forgive your giving me such a turn."

Splendid, my grandmother, wasn't she, with her poor little Monsieur Alcide?

Next day she went and found him a hiding-place at Meudon.

One wouldn't have thought the daughter of Dussuel the philosopher a very likely subject to believe in miracles, or to have hazarded a very near approach to the confines of the unseen world. She hadn't a particle of religion in her composition, and anything in the shape of a mystery used to revolt her somewhat hard common sense. Nevertheless, level-headed and practical as she was, she was never tired of recounting the details of a marvellous incident of which she had been an eye-witness.

When visiting her father during his detention in the Franciscan convent at Versailles, she had become acquainted with Madame de Laville, who was a prisoner there. On her release the latter went to reside in the Rue de Lancry, in the same house as my grandmother. The two sets of rooms opened on to the same landing.

Madame de Laville used to live with her younger sister, whose name was Amélie.

G

Amélie was a lovely, tall creature. Her pale
face, enshrined in a setting of dusky hair, had an
expression of incomparable beauty; and her eyes,
now languorous, now sparkling with fire, always
appeared to be seeking something mysterious and
unknown.

Amélie, who, while waiting an opportunity of
settling down in the world, had become a lay-
canoness in the Community of l'Argentière, was
reported, when little more than a child, to have
endured uncomplainingly the pangs of unrequited
love.

She appeared to be weighed down with ennui.
Occasionally she would burst into a flood of tears
without apparent cause. Sometimes she would
remain for days together in a state of dejection,
at others she would feverishly devour her books
of devotion. A prey to her own delusions, she
would writhe in unspeakable agony.

Her sister's arrest, the dreadful fate that had
befallen many of her friends who had been dragged
to the guillotine as conspirators, and the alarm
to which she was incessantly a prey, completed the
ruin of her already impaired constitution. She
grew terribly emaciated. The drums which daily
beat the sections to arms, the companies of citizens
that filed past her window wearing red caps, armed
with pikes, and singing the *Ça ira!* threw her into

a state of terror that was followed alternately by fits of stupor and exaltation. Nervous attacks ensued that were terrible in their intensity, and gave rise to remarkable effects.

Amélie was visited by dreams and visions so vivid, that those to whom she related them were filled with amazement.

Wandering about by night, sometimes waking, sometimes in a trance, far-off sounds assailed her ear—the sighs and groans of the victims of the guillotine. Sometimes standing erect, she would stretch forth her arm, and, pointing to some form in the gloom, visible to none but herself, she would utter the name of Robespierre. "Her forebodings always come true," her sister used to say, "and she can tell when evil is at hand."

During the night of the 9th Thermidor my grandmother and her father sat up with the two sisters in their room. All four were in a state of great agitation, summing up the grave events that had taken place during the day, and striving to foretell what would come of them. A decree had been passed ordering the tyrant's arrest ; he had been taken to the Luxembourg, where the concierge had refused to receive him. From there he had been conveyed to the *Bureau de Police* on the *Quai des Orfèvres*, then handed over by the Commune and removed to the *Hôtel de Ville*. . . . Was he still there? And how was he bearing himself? Was he cowed or defiant? All four were consumed with anxiety, but no sound reached their ears save ever and anon the clatter of Henriot's messengers as they galloped past in fiery haste along the street. Thus they sat waiting, and waiting, reviving old memories, exchanging hopes and fears.

Amélie alone was silent.

Suddenly she uttered a piercing shriek.

It was half-past one in the morning. Leaning over a mirror, she seemed to be witnessing the enactment of some tragic scene.

"I see him," she said; "I see him. Ah! how pale he looks! Blood is pouring from his mouth! His teeth and his jaws are shattered! Praise be to God! He who has drunk so deep of the blood of others shall now drink but of his own."

As she finished these words, which she uttered in weird, chanting tones, she gave vent to a cry of horror, and fell backwards with a crash. She had fallen into a swoon.

It was at that very moment, in the Council Chamber of the *Hôtel de Ville*, that Robespierre was struck by the pistol shot which shattered his jaw, and put an end to the Reign of Terror.

My grandmother, though a freethinker, firmly believed in this vision.

You ask me how I explain it? Well, then, my grandmother, sceptic though she was, held a pretty strong belief in the Devil and the Black Bogey. When she was young, the necromantic art amused her; but later on she took fright at the Devil. But it was too late; he held her fast, and she had to believe in him.

After the 9th of Thermidor, life once more became tolerable for the little group in the Rue de Lancry. My grandmother was highly delighted at this change in the aspect of affairs; but it was not in her nature to bear malice against the Revolutionaries. She did not admire them—she never admired anybody but me—but she did not hate them. It never entered her head to call them to account for the frights they had given her; and perhaps the explanation is, that they never really *did* frighten her. But the main reason was that my grandmother was "true blue," and, as someone has said, "once a blue always a blue."

Meanwhile, Danger was pursuing his brilliant career on many a field of battle. His star was always in the ascendant, and he was leading his brigade in full-dress uniform at the glorious skirmish of Abensberg, when he was struck by a cannon ball and killed.

It was from the columns of the *Moniteur* that my grandmother learned that she was a widow, and that the gallant General Danger had fallen covered with laurels.

"How unfortunate!" she exclaimed; "a fine-looking man like that, too." The following year she married Monsieur Hippolyte Nozière, head-clerk at the *Ministère de la Justice*, an open-hearted, jovial man, who played the flute from six till nine in the morning, and from five to eight in the evening. This time the match was an entire success. They were in love with each other, and, not being very young, they were able to bear with each other's foibles. Caroline forgave Hippolyte his everlasting flute, and Hippolyte put up with Caroline's little whims and fancies. They were happy.

My grandfather Nozière was the author of a *Statistique des Prisons* (Paris, Imprimerie Royal, 1817–19, 2 vols., 4to); and of *Les Filles de Momus chansons nouvelles* (Paris, privately printed, 1821, 18mo).

He suffered tortures from gout; but the gout couldn't damp his spirits, even when it put a stop to his flute-playing. In the end it choked him. I never knew him; but that's his portrait, over there—the man in the blue coat with his hair in little curls like a lamb's fleece, and his chin buried in an enormous cravat.

"I shall feel his loss to my dying day," my

grandmother used to say at eighty, when she had been a widow for fifteen years.

"And well you may, madame," replied an old friend of ours; "Nozière had all the virtues that go to make a good husband."

"All the virtues and all the defects, please," rejoined my grandmother.

" To be an ideal husband, then, a man must have defects ! "

" Pardi ! " cried my grandmother, with a shrug. " He must have no vices, and that in itself is a great defect ! "

She died on the 4th July 1853, in her eighty-first year.

IV

THE TOOTH

F people took as much pains to keep in the background, as they do to bring themselves into prominence, they would avoid a deal of trouble. Of this truth I had early experience.

It was a wet day. Someone had made me a present of a postillion's outfit—cap, whip, reins, and bells—everything complete. There were plenty of bells. I put to—that is to say, I harnessed myself to myself, for I was postillion, horses, and carriage all in one. My portion of road extended from the kitchen to the dining-room, along a passage. The dining-room, I found, did splendidly for a village; and the mahogany sideboard, where I changed horses, was the very thing for the *White Horse Inn*. The passage was the highway, with its ever-shifting views and unlooked-for encounters. The space to which I was restricted was cramped and dark, yet my delight was as great as if a limitless horizon lay before me; and within these walls, which I knew so well, I met with those unexpected incidents on which the charm of travelling depends. The reason was that I was a great magician in those days. It is a gift I have since had the misfortune to lose ; but on that rainy day, when I was playing postillions, I possessed it in abundance.

The fact that such a gift was mine ought to have satisfied me, but is one ever satisfied ? I wanted people to see me ; I wanted to take them by surprise, to dazzle them, to astonish them. My velvet cap and my bells would be nothing worth if there were no one to admire them, and, as I heard my father and mother talking together in the next room, I dashed in making a great noise. My father looked at me for a second or two in silence, then, with a shrug, he said, " The child doesn't know what to do with himself here. We shall have to send him to school."

" He's only a little boy, yet," replied my mother.

" Well," said my father, " he will be put with the little boys."

All this I understood perfectly well ; but what followed I could not catch, and if I am able to set down everything clearly here it is because I have heard about it all so often since.

" The child has no brothers or sisters, and he is getting into a dreamy way that will do him harm in after years. Solitude over-excites his imagination, and I have already noticed that his head is

full of fanciful ideas. But the children of his own
age with whom he will mix at school will give him
a notion of what the world is like. He will learn
from them what men are. He cannot learn it
from you and me, for he looks upon us as tutelary
genii. His school companions, on the other hand,
will be his equals. Some will excite his compassion,
and he will learn to take their part ; others he will
have to win over or to fight. In this manner he
will serve his apprenticeship to life."

" But are you not afraid, dear, that some of the
children will be naughty ? "

" Even they will be of use to him if he is
intelligent," replied my father, " for he will learn to
distinguish them from the good children, and that
is a highly necessary piece of knowledge. Besides,
you can go yourself and see what sort of schools
there are about here, and choose one where the
children have been brought up in the same way as
Pierre. The nature of man is everywhere the same,
but their nurture varies greatly according to the
locality. Careful cultivation carried on for several
generations will produce a flower of extreme delicacy,
and this flower, which has cost a century to produce,
may wither in a few days. Uncultivated children
would without profit to themselves exert a de-
teriorating influence on the culture of our child.
Noble thoughts are the gift of God. Noble ways

are learned from example, and become implanted by inheritance. The possession of noble ways is finer than the possession of a noble name; for the former is natural, and its own grace is its patent; the title-deeds of the latter are old papers that one has much ado to read."

"You are quite right, dear," said my mother; "and to-morrow I will begin to look out for a school. I will be guided in my choice by what you say, and I will take care that the school is doing well financially, for money troubles distract a master's thoughts and spoil his temper. What do you think, dear, of a dame's school?"

My father did not answer.

"What do you think of the idea?" repeated my mother.

"It is a matter that requires consideration," said my father.

He was sitting in his arm-chair at his roll-top desk, and for some minutes had been looking intently at a kind of little bone, one end of which was pointed, and the other rough and eaten away. He was turning it over in his fingers, and he was clearly turning it over in his mind as well; and thenceforth, for all my bells, he was oblivious of my existence. My mother was leaning over the back of his chair, and her thoughts were still running on what she had just been saying.

The doctor showed her the ugly little bone,
saying, "This is the tooth of a man who lived in
the time of the mammoths, in the ice age; of a
man who dwelt in a cave once bare and desolate,
but now half hidden with wild grape and gilly-
flowers, the cave near which has stood, for many
years now, that pretty white house in which we
sojourned for two summer months the year we were
married. Two happy months were they! There
was an old piano there, and all day long you used
to play Mozart, and, thanks to you, that winged,
winsome music took flight through the windows, and
brought joy into the valley where the cave-dweller
had only heard the tiger's howl.

"This man knew nought, save fear and hunger.
He resembled a brute beast. His forehead was
low. When he scowled, the muscles of his eyebrows produced hideous wrinkles; his cheek-bones
formed two great protuberances upon his face; his
teeth projected from his mouth. Look at this one;
see how long and pointed it is!

"Such was primeval man. But, imperceptibly,
by dint of long and splendid effort, man became
less wretched, and, therefore, less ferocious. The
habit of thought developed his brain, and his forehead grew larger. Being no longer employed in
rending raw flesh, his teeth became shorter and
his jawbone less massive. Yes, the human face

became transfigured with a glorious beauty, and upon woman's lips there dawned a smile."

At this point my father kissed my mother on the cheek, and my mother smiled; and then, slowly raising the tooth of the cave-man above his head, he apostrophised it thus:

"Man of a bygone age, thou, whose rude and savage relic I hold here in my hand, the thoughts of thee stir me to my being's inmost depths. I respect thee, O my ancestor, and I love thee. Accept, in that unfathomable Past where thou dost slumber, the homage of my gratitude, for I know the debt I owe thee. I know from what depths of wretchedness thy efforts have preserved me. True, thy thoughts were not of the future; true, but a feeble glimmer of intelligence flickered within the darkness of thy soul. Still, thou wert man—some dim and vague idea impelled thee onward toward the attainment of what is fair and good in men's eyes. Thou didst live in misery, but thou didst not live in vain. Thou didst bestow raiment upon woman, and men learned the price of beauty."

Here, my father replaced the prehistoric tooth upon his secretaire, and embraced my mother.

Then he began again. "Thus," said he, "to these ancestors we are indebted for everything—for everything—even for love."

I thought I should like to touch this tooth that

had inspired my father to utter things beyond my comprehension, and I went up to the desk to lay hold of it; but, at the sound of my bells, my father turned his head in my direction, and said :

"But, stay, the task is not yet over. We should be showing ourselves less generous than the cavemen if, now that our turn has come, we did not strive to make life better and more secure for our children than it is for ourselves. To achieve this end, two things are indispensable : knowledge and love; for with knowledge and love the world is made."

"No doubt, dear," said my mother; "but the more I think about it, the more thoroughly I am convinced that a little boy like our Pierre ought to be under a woman's care. I have heard a good deal about a certain demoiselle Lefort; I will go and see her to-morrow."

V

MY FIRST ACQUAINTANCE WITH POETRY

ADEMOISELLE LEFORT, who kept a school for little children in the Faubourg Saint Germain, consented to receive me as a pupil from ten to twelve in the morning, and from two to four in the afternoon. I had formed the most dreadful notions about this school in my own mind, and when my nurse dragged me there for the first time, I gave myself up for lost.

I was therefore extremely surprised, on entering, to find a large room with five or six little girls and about a dozen little boys in it, all laughing, making grimaces, and generally displaying their unconcern.

On the other hand, I perceived that Mademoiselle Lefort wore an expression of profound melancholy. Her blue eyes were moist, and her lips slightly apart.

Pallid-looking side-curls hung down each side of her face like the willow boughs that droop mournfully over the edge of a stream; and she gazed straight in front of her without seeing anything, apparently lost in a dream.

The harmless aspect of this afflicted spinster, and the liveliness of the children, gave me confidence; and the idea that I was going to share the lot of several little girls gradually put the last of my fears to flight.

Mademoiselle Lefort, having given me a slate and pencil, made me sit down beside a bright-eyed, sharp-looking boy of my own age.

"My name's Fontanet," he said; "what's yours?"

He then asked me what my father was, and I told him a doctor.

"Mine's a lawyer," replied Fontanet; "that's better."

"Why?" said I.

"What! you don't see why it's better to be a lawyer?"

"No."

"Then you must be a silly!"

Fontanet had a resourceful mind. He advised me to keep silkworms, and showed me a fine multiplication table he had made all by himself. This excited my admiration. Fables were all I knew about.

When I went home, Mademoiselle Lefort gave me a good mark, which I couldn't discover the use of at all. My mother explained that lack of usefulness was the distinctive characteristic of all

honours. She then wanted to know what I had
done during my first day at school. I told her I
had looked at Mademoiselle Lefort.

She laughed at me, but I had spoken the truth.
I have, in fact, always been inclined to regard life
as a spectacle. I have never been, properly speaking, an observer, for an observer must have a
system to guide him, and I have none. The
observer, moreover, chooses his field, whereas in the
case of the spectator his eyes choose for him. I am
a born sightseer, and all my life long I believe I
shall retain the unsophisticated outlook, the ingenuousness, that marks those town-bred loungers
who find amusement in everything, and who still
display, when other folk are only thinking about
"getting on," the disinterested curiosity of little
children. Of all the spectacles of which I have
been a beholder, the only ones that have bored me
are those which are presented to our gaze on the
stage at the theatre. On the other hand, dramas
in real life, beginning with those enacted at Mademoiselle Lefort's Academy, have always afforded me
plenty of entertainment.

But to continue. I went on scrutinising my
schoolmistress, and the idea that she was melancholy
obtained such a hold on my mind that I asked
Fontanet if he could tell me why she looked so sad.
Fontanet, without committing himself to any definite

H

statement, was disposed to ascribe it to remorse. He had a great idea that he remembered seeing the outward signs of melancholy suddenly manifest themselves on Mademoiselle's countenance on the day, already remote, when she had, without any justification whatever, confiscated his boxwood top, proceeding almost immediately thereafter to make him the victim of a further outrage, for, in order to stifle the complaints of him whom she had despoiled, she rammed the dunce's cap right down over his head.

Fontanet was of opinion that a soul which bore the stain of such deeds as these would have said farewell for ever to joy and repose. Fontanet's reasons, however, did not satisfy me, and I endeavoured to think what else it could be.

But, to tell the truth, it was no easy matter to think at all in Mademoiselle Lefort's class-room, because of the incessant uproar that went on there. The pupils would engage in pitched battles before the very eyes of the visible yet absent Mademoiselle Lefort. We used to throw so many catechisms and crusts of bread at one another, that the air was darkened with them, and the class-room filled with a perpetual racket. The only quiet ones were the very youngest children, who sat with their tongues out and their feet in their hands, gazing upwards at the ceiling and smiling placidly.

Suddenly, Mademoiselle Lefort, with the air of one walking in her sleep, would enter the fray, chastise someone who didn't deserve it, and then shut herself up again in her melancholy, as though in a tower. Try, please, to realise what must have been the state of mind of a little boy of eight who, amid all this incomprehensible tumult, had been doing nothing for six weeks but write on a slate :

"To his grave, unheeded, Malfilâtre by hunger was driven."

That was my task. Now and again I used to clasp my head in my hands in order to collect my ideas ; but of these ideas only one was at all distinct, and that was, the melancholy of Mademoiselle Lefort. My thoughts were perpetually occupied with my grief-stricken schoolmistress. Fontanet used to relate weird stories that still further whetted my curiosity. He said that, every morning, when you went by her door, you would hear doleful cries mingled with the clanking of chains. " I remember," he added, " that, a long time ago—it might be a month—she read out to the whole class a story which they thought was in poetry, and that she sobbed all the time."

There was something about Fontanet's tale that went right through me, and an event occurred the next day which led me to think that it was not altogether imaginary—at least, so far as the reading

aloud was concerned. As for the chains that made
Fontanet grow pale, I never found out anything
about them, and I now take it that the noise of
these alleged chains was in reality the rattle of the
poker and tongs.

But this is what happened next day. Mademoiselle Lefort rapped on her table with a ruler for
silence, coughed, and said in a sepulchral voice :

PooR JEANNE !

Then, after a pause, she added :

" Jeanne was the fairest of the village maids."

Fontanet gave me a dig in the ribs with his elbow,
and exploded with laughter. Mademoiselle Lefort
flashed an indignant glance at him, and then, in
tones more gloomy than the penitential psalms,
went on with the tale of Poor Jeanne. It is
probable, nay certain, that the story was in verse
from beginning to end ; but, of course, I can only
tell it as I remember it, and I trust that the *disjecta
membra* of the poem will be discernible in my prose.

Jeanne was betrothed. She had plighted her
troth to a gallant young mountaineer. Oswald was
the lucky herdsman's name. And now all was
ready for the bridal morn, and Jeanne's companions
had brought her the wreath and the veil. Ah !
happy Jeanne ! But, alas, she went off into a de-

cline. The pallor of death overspread her cheeks.
Oswald came down from the mountain and hastened
to her side, crying, "Art thou not for ever mine?"
But she, in faint and far-off tones, replied, "Dear
Oswald, farewell; I am dying." Poor Jeanne!
The tomb was her bridal bed, and the bells of the
village church, which should have rung out for her
wedding, tolled sadly for her burial.

The story contained a large number of words
then heard by me for the first time, the meaning of
which I did not understand. But the whole appeared to me to be so sad and so beautiful, that I was
conscious as I listened to it, of a thrill I had never
felt before. The charm that belongs to melancholy was revealed to me by thirty lines or so of
verse whose literal meaning I should have been
totally unable to explain; but except when one is
old, one need not understand much in order to feel
a great deal. The obscure may be touching, and
it is eminently true that the youthful mind finds
pleasure in the undefined. Tears welled up from
my overburdened heart, and neither by grimaces
nor by jeers could Fontanet put an end to my
sobbing. Still, I had no doubts at that time of
Fontanet's superiority. Not till he became an
Under-Secretary of State was I visited by an un-
certainty about the matter.

My tears were pleasing in the sight of Made-

moiselle Lefort.   She called me to her and
said :

" Pierre Nozière, you have wept; here is the
cross of honour.   Know that I it was who wrote
that poem.   I have a large notebook filled with
verses just as beautiful as those ; but, as yet, I
have not found a publisher to print them.   Is not
that a horrible, nay, an unconscionable thing ? "

" Oh ! mademoiselle ! " said I ; " I am so glad.
Now I know the cause of your distress.   You loved
poor Jeanne who lies dead in the hamlet, and it
is because you are thinking of her, is it not, that
you are sad and never notice what goes on in the
class ? "

Unfortunately, these observations displeased her,
for she looked at me wrathfully, and said :

" Jeanne is a fiction.   You are a little silly.
Give me that cross and go back to your place."

I went back to my place weeping.   This time
it was on my own account that I wept, and I
confess that these fresh tears had not that sensation
of sweetness that had mingled with those poor
Jeanne had wrung from me.   There was another
thing, too, that increased my distress.   I had not
the slightest idea what a fiction was.   Fontanet was
just as ignorant as I.

I asked my mother about it when I got home.

" A fiction," said my mother, " is a lie."

"Oh ! mamma !" said I, "what a pity that Jeanne was a lie."

" Jeanne, which Jeanne ? " asked my mother.

" Jeanne was the fairest of the village maids,"

and I recounted what I remembered of the story.

My mother said nothing to me, but I heard her whisper in my father's ear :

" What wretched stuff this child is being taught !"

"Wretched stuff, indeed," replied my father ; " but what do you expect an old maid to know of pedagogy ? I have an educational system which I will explain to you in detail some day. According to this system, we should instruct a child of our Pierre's age in the habits of the animals which he resembles in inclination and intelligence. Pierre is capable of understanding the faithfulness of the dog, the unselfishness of the elephants, the trickery of the monkey. That is the kind of thing they ought to talk to him about, instead of this Jeanne, this village, and these bells, which have no common sense about them."

" You are right," replied my mother. " Children and animals understand one another very well ; they are both close to Nature. But, believe me, dear, there is something that children understand even better than monkeys and their tricks : I mean the noble deeds of great men. Heroism is as plain as daylight, even to a little boy, and if Pierre were told about the death of the Chevalier d'Assas, he would, with God's aid, understand it as well as you or I."

"Alas!" said my father, with a sigh, "I believe, on the contrary, that there are divers conflicting ideas regarding the nature of heroism, and that they vary with the age, the place, and the people. But that is of no importance. What does matter in a deed of self-sacrifice is the sacrifice. Though the object for which we sacrifice our lives may be an illusion, the sacrifice itself is none the less a reality, and this reality is the most splendid adornment that man can embellish his moral wretchedness withal. Dear heart, your natural generosity has enabled you to comprehend these truths better than I with all my experience and study could comprehend them. I shall incorporate them in my system."

Thus did the doctor and my mother discuss matters.

A week later I was writing on my slate for the last time amid the tumult:

"To his grave, unheeded, Malfilâtre by hunger was driven."

Fontanet and I both quitted Mademoiselle Lefort's Academy on the same day.

VI

TEUTOBOCHUS

I T does not seem possible to me that a man should have an altogether common cast of mind whose young days were passed round about the quays of Paris, hard by the Palais Mazarin, where the eye looks across to the Louvre and the Tuileries, and where the glorious River Seine flows on amid the towers and turrets and spires of Old Paris. From the Rue Guénégaud to the Rue du Bac the shops of the booksellers, antiquaries, and printsellers are full to overflowing of the fairest forms of art, and the most curious relics of the past. With its quaint elegance and comic confusion, every shop window is a lure for eye and mind. Whoso examines them with the seeing eye always carries some thought away with him, even as a bird flies off with a wisp of straw for its nest.

And, since there are trees there, and books, and since women come and go thereby, there is surely no fairer place in all the world.

In my childhood days this curio market abounded

(much more so than it does at present) with old
furniture, old prints, old books, and old pictures,
carved credence tables, china jugs, enamels,
coloured pottery, orphreys, figured stuffs, tapestry
pictures, illuminated books, and many a rare *editio
princeps* bound in choice morocco. These delectable
wares were freely displayed for sale to the gaze of
the learned and discriminating collector, who, as
yet, was immune from the rivalry of stockbrokers
and actresses. They were already familiar to
Fontanet and me when we were still going about
in wide lace collars, knickerbockers, and short
socks.

Fontanet used to live at the corner of the Rue
Bonaparte, where his father had his chambers. The
house where my parents dwelt adjoined one of the
wings of the Hôtel de Chimay. We were friends
and neighbours, Fontanet and I. Whenever we had
a holiday, we used to go and play in the Tuileries
together, making our way along this learned Quai
Voltaire. And as we went along, with hoops in
our hands and balls in our jacket pockets, we used
to look in the shops just as the old gentlemen did,
and formed our own ideas concerning all those
strange things that had come down from the Past,
—the dim, mysterious Past.

Ah ! yes, we sauntered about in proper style,
we hovered round the book-stalls, we weighed the

merits of the prints, for all the world like a pair of accomplished connoisseurs.

It all interested us greatly, but Fontanet, I must avow, did not share my respect for everything that was old. He used to laugh at the queer mediæval shaving-dishes or at holy bishops who had lost their noses. Even in those days Fontanet was the same go-ahead, dashing fellow whom you have heard addressing the Chamber of Deputies. His irreverence used to send a shiver down my back; I didn't like to hear him refer to an ancestral portrait as an "ugly phiz." I was a conservative, and I have still got some of my conservatism left; and all my philosophy has not deprived me of my affection for old trees and country curés.

There is yet another thing in which I differ from Fontanet, and that is my inclination to admire what I don't understand. I used to adore books on the occult, and everything—or nearly everything—was occult to me then. Fontanet, on the other hand, would only admire a thing in proportion as he was acquainted with its uses. "See," he used to say, "there's a hinge there, that opens"; or, "Look, there's a screw, that comes off." Fontanet had a balanced mind—he was level-headed. I must add, though, that he could grow quite enthusiastic over the picture of a battle. "The Passage of the Beresina" really moved him. We were deeply interested,

too, in the armourer's shop. One day we saw
Monsieur Petit-Prêtre, surrounded by lances,
targets, breastplates, and bucklers, and wearing his
green baize apron, get up and go off limping, like
Vulcan himself, to the other end of his shop to
fetch an antique sword, which he proceeded to fix
in an iron vice on his bench to clean the blade and
repair the hilt ; and then we knew that we were
witnessing a noble sight. Monsieur Petit-Prêtre
seemed to tower a hundred cubits above us. We
remained speechless with admiration, our faces glued
to the window. Fontanet's black eyes sparkled, and
his dark, intelligent little face beamed all over with
excitement.

The recollection of what we had seen greatly
elated us that evening, and countless enthusiastic
plans began to take shape in our brains.

"Suppose," said Fontanet, "suppose we get
some of that silver paper they wrap up chocolates
with, and make some armour like that which Petit-
Prêtre has in his shop."

It was a fine idea. But we were not so successful in carrying it out as we had hoped. I made
a helmet, but Fontanet took it for a wizard's cap.

And so I said : "Let's start a museum !"

The idea was excellent, but at the moment we
had nothing to put in the museum but half a
hundred marbles and a dozen tops or so.

It was at this point that Fontanet came out with yet a third plan: "Let's compose a History of France," he exclaimed, "with all the details, in fifty volumes."

This proposal fairly enchanted me. I clapped my hands and shouted for joy. We arranged to begin the following morning, although we had a page of the *De Viris* to get up.

"All the details!" said Fontanet once more; "we must put in all the details."

That was precisely my idea of the thing—we would have all the details.

We had to go to bed, but I stayed awake a good quarter of an hour, so excited was I by the sublime idea of writing a History of France in fifty volumes, with all the details.

Well, we began our History. I can't for the life of me tell why it was we began with King Teutobochus, but our plan required it. Our first chapter brought us face to face with this King Teutobochus, who was thirty feet tall—a fact you can demonstrate by measuring his bones, which have been accidentally unearthed. Fancy having to face a giant like that at the very outset. The encounter was terrible. Even Fontanet was staggered.

"We shall have to skip old Teutobochus," said he.

But I did not dare.

The History of France in fifty volumes stopped short at Teutobochus.

Alas! how often in my life have I engaged in this adventure of the Giant and the Book. How often, when on the point of beginning a great work, undertaking a vast enterprise, have I been pulled up sharp by a Teutobochus, whom the vulgar call Fate, or Chance, or Necessity. I have come now to calling down blessings on all those Teutobochuses who, shutting me out from the hazardous paths of glory, have left me to the care of those two faithful guardians: Obscurity and Mediocrity. Gentle and kind to me are they both, and they love me well. Surely it is meet that I should return their love.

As for Fontanet, my subtle crony Fontanet—barrister, judge, director of divers companies, and a Deputy to boot—it is wonderful to see how freely he disports himself and runs in and out between the legs of all the Teutobochuses of public life. Had I been in his place, I should have smashed my nose against them times without number.

VII

THE PRESTIGE OF THE ABBÉ JUBAL

IT was with a heart overflowing with awe and pride that I made my début in the Lower Eighth. The professor, Monsieur l'Abbé Jubal, was not, in himself, a formidable individual. He did not seem harsh ; indeed, he had rather a young-ladylike air about him. But he sat in a great, high, black chair, and that made him redoubtable in my sight. His voice and expression were gentle. He had curly hair, white hands, and a kindly disposition. He was like a sheep, the resemblance being perhaps rather greater than was becoming in a professor.

My mother saw him one day in the parlour, and murmured, " He is very young " ; and she said it in a tone of conviction.

I was just succeeding in ceasing to be afraid of him when I found myself constrained to yield him my admiration. It came about while I was repeating my "prep.," some lines of the Abbé Gauthier on the early kings of France.

I delivered myself of every line at one breath, as if it were composed of a single word :

" Pharamondfutdit-onlepremierdecesrois
QuelesFrancsdanslaGauleontmissurlepavois
ClodionprendCambraipuisrègneMérovée." . . .

There I stopped short, and repeated *Mérovée*, *Mérovée*, *Mérovée*. This rhyme, uniting usefulness with charm, reminded me that when the throne was filled by *Méroveé*, *Lutèce* was *préservée*. . . . But from what ? That, it was quite impossible for me to tell, for it had completely slipped my memory. To tell the truth, I hadn't been very much impressed by the affair. I had an idea that *Lutèce* was an old lady. I was glad she had been saved ; but, on the whole, my interest in her affairs was extremely small. Unfortunately, Monsieur l'Abbé Jubal appeared to be very anxious that I should say what she had been saved from. I kept stammering " Er—Er—*Mérovée*/ . . . Er—Er—Er." I would have said, " I'll give it up ! " if it had been the thing in the Lower Eighth. Fontanet kept jeering at me, and Monsieur Jubal began to pare his nails.

" ' Des fureurs d'Attila Lutèce est préservée,' "

he said at last. " As you had forgotten the line,

you should have made up something, instead of
stopping short like that.   You could say :

or,
      ' De l'invasion d'Attila Lutèce est préservée ' ;

      ' Du sombre Attila Lutèce est préservée ' ;

or, more elegantly,

      ' Du fléau de Dieu, Lutèce est préservée.'

You can alter the words so long as you retain the
metre."

I got a bad mark ; but Monsieur l'Abbé Jubal
acquired immense prestige in my eyes by reason of
his poetic facility.   This prestige was shortly to
become greater still.

Monsieur Jubal, though his duties kept him pretty
close to Noel and Chapsal's Grammar and the Abbé
Gauthier's History of France, did not neglect the
moral and religious side of our education.

One day—I don't remember what had led up to
it—he put on a grave air and said :

"My sons, if you were called upon to entertain
a Minister of State, you would be anxious to do
him the honours of your house, as being the representative of the sovereign.   Well, then, what
respect ought you not to pay to priests who are
God's representatives on earth.   Just as far as God
is above kings, so far is the priest above Ministers
of State."

I had never entertained a Minister, and I didn't expect to do so for a long time to come. Moreover, I knew perfectly well that, if one did happen to come to our house, my mother would send me to have dinner with the servants, as, I am sorry to say, she always did, when we had a dinner party. Nevertheless I fully understood that priests were a prodigiously respectable class, and, applying this truth to Monsieur Jubal, I grew very troubled in my heart. I recollected that I had, in his presence, pinned a Dancing Jack on to Fontanet's back. Was that a respectful thing to do? Should I have pinned a Dancing Jack on to Fontanet's back if a Minister had been there? Assuredly not. Yet here had I been pinning on this thing, certainly without the knowledge, but still in the presence of, Monsieur Jubal, who was so far above any Minister of State. Nay, more, the wretched thing was sticking out its tongue!

Now the light had illumined my soul, and I was consumed with remorse. I made up my mind to honour Monsieur l'Abbé Jubal, and if, since then, I have occasionally dropped pebbles down Fontanet's neck in class time, and drawn caricatures on the chair of Monsieur l'Abbé Jubal himself, I have at all events done these things with the full consciousness of the enormity of my misdeeds.

Some short time after this, an event occurred

which enabled me to realise the spiritual greatness
of Monsieur l'Abbé Jubal.

I was in chapel with two or three other boys,
waiting my turn to confess. The twilight shades
were falling. The glow of the sanctuary lamp was
tremulously reflected by the golden stars that
twinkled in the gloom of the vaulted roof. At the
far end of the choir the painted statue of the Virgin
seemed to float dim and unsubstantial as a vision.
The altar was laden with gilt vases filled with
flowers, and the air was fragrant with incense.
Countless objects glimmered indistinctly in the
gathering dusk, and even ennui, that dread malady
of childhood, took on a gracious aspect; and it
seemed to me that just beyond the sanctuary lay
Paradise itself.

It grew quite dark. Suddenly I beheld Monsieur
l'Abbé Jubal, with a lantern in his hand, proceed
along the aisle as far as the choir. He made a
profound genuflexion, and then, opening the
sanctuary gate, he ascended the steps of the altar.
I watched intently. He undid a parcel and took
out some wreaths of artificial flowers, which resembled those close-packed bunches of cherries
that old women hawk about the streets in July.
And I was filled with wonder as I beheld my professor draw near to the altar of the Blessed Virgin.
I watched you, Monsieur l'Abbé, I watched you

pick up some tin-tacks with your finger and thumb,
and put them in your mouth. I feared, for a
moment, that you were going to swallow them;
but no; it was merely that you wanted to have
them within easy reach. Then, mounting a form,
you set to work to nail up the wreaths round about
the niche of the Blessed Virgin. But from time
to time you descended from your form in order
that you might judge how your work appeared
from a distance, and you saw that it was good.
Your cheeks glowed; your eyes sparkled. You
would have smiled, had it not been for the tin-
tacks in your mouth. And I—I looked on at you
in whole-hearted admiration. And, though the
lantern on the ground lit up your nostrils in comic
fashion, I deemed you had an imposing mien. I
recognised that, as you had led us to infer in an
ingenious speech, you were more exalted than
Ministers of State. It seemed to me that to ride
forth to victory in dazzling uniform, and mounted
upon a white charger, was not so splendid an
achievement as hanging wreaths on a chapel wall.
I felt that my vocation was to imitate you, and
imitate you I did, that same night, at home; for,
getting hold of all the paper I could find, I cut it
up into strips with my mother's scissors, and made
it into wreaths. My home lessons suffered con-
siderably, the French grammar exercise being

particularly unfortunate. The exercise in question was taken from the manual of one Monsieur Coquempot. That book was a cruel book, yet I harbour no ill-will against its author, and, if he had borne a less haunting patronymic, I would have generously forgotten him. But, Coquempot! You don't forget a name like that! Far be it from me to take an ungenerous advantage of this purely accidental circumstance. At the same time, I hope I may be permitted to express my astonishment that it should be necessary to do such painful exercises in order to learn what is commonly called one's mother-tongue. Indeed, I could learn it very well from my mother, merely by hearing her talk. For she talked enchantingly, did my mother!

But Monsieur l'Abbé Jubal thought there was nobody like Coquempot, and as my excuses failed to convince him, he gave me a bad mark. The school year went by without any noteworthy incident. Fontanet went in for breeding caterpillars in his desk; so I, not to be outdone, did the same, although I loathed the things. Now Fontanet hated Coquempot, too, and this formed a bond of union between us. At the mere mention of the name "Coquempot," we exchanged significant glances from our respective seats, and pulled wry faces. That was how we gave vent to our pent-up feelings. Fontanet told me for a fact that, if they

went on doing Coquempot in the Eighth, he would
run away and get a berth as cabin-boy on a liner.
I liked the notion, and I promised Fontanet I would
join with him.   We swore eternal friendship.

When speech-day came, Fontanet and I were
unrecognisable ; you wouldn't have known us—
probably because we had had our hair brushed.
Our brand new jackets and white trousers, the
drugget, the crowd of relations, the flower-bedecked
daïs, all filled me with excited expectancy. The
books and the crowns made a brilliant pile, and I
looked with eager anxiety to see if I could make
out what I was to receive ; and I trembled as I sat
in my seat. Fontanet was more sensible. He
made no effort to probe the future. Indeed, he
maintained a magnificent imperturbability. Turning
his little ferret-face about in every direction, he
noted the comical noses of the papas and the
ridiculous hats of the mammas with an insouciance
quite beyond me.

The band struck up; the Principal, wearing his
little ceremonial tippet over his soutane, made his
appearance on the daïs, accompanied by a general
in full-dress uniform, and followed by the whole
professorial staff. I recognised them all. They
took their places behind the general according to
their rank. First came the Vice-Principal, then the
professors of the senior classes, then Monsieur

Schuwer, the music master, Monsieur Trouillon, the writing master, and Sergeant Morin, the gymnastic instructor. Monsieur l'Abbé Jubal brought up the rear, and deposited himself on a miserable little stool, which, for want of room, only had three legs on the daïs, and was boring a hole in the drugget with the fourth. Even this humble place Monsieur l'Abbé Jubal was not fated to retain very long. Fresh arrivals came, and he was thrust into a corner, where he disappeared from view beneath a flag. Then, somebody put a table on the top of him, and that completed the business. Fontanet was highly amused at this final eclipse, but I was dumfounded to see so great an authority on flowers and poetry, a representative of God upon earth, left in a corner as though he were of no more account than a stick or umbrella.

VIII

FONTANET'S CAP

VERY Saturday we used to be taken to confession. If anyone can tell me why, I shall be glad. It was a practice that I regarded with considerable awe and no little misgiving. I do not think that Monsieur l'Aumônier took any genuine interest in listening to the recital of my misdeeds, and it was unquestionably very unpleasant for me to have to tell him about them. The first difficulty was to find them. You may perhaps believe me when I tell you that, when I was ten, I did not possess the gift of self-analysis in a sufficiently marked degree to enable me to make a thorough examination of my inner consciousness. But no sins meant no confession; so sins had to be found. True, I had been presented with a little manual, a sort of compendium of all the sins. It was therefore merely a matter of selection, but even that presented difficulties. There was such a multitude of dark and difficult references to larceny, simony, prevarication, fornication, concupiscence!

In it I found this sort of thing: "I am guilty of having given way to despair"; "I have been guilty of listening to evil conversations." All that I found very perplexing.

For this reason I usually kept to the section which dealt with "Inattention," "Inattention in church," "Inattention at meals," "Inattention at meetings." I confessed to all, and felt terribly ashamed of the bankrupt condition of my conscience.

I was humiliated at not having any real sins. But at last, one day, I thought of Fontanet's cap. I had got my sin! I was saved!

From that day onwards, as sure as Saturday came round, I relieved my soul of the burden of Fontanet's cap, and laid it at the feet of my confessor. When I reflected how, by the damage I had wrought this cap, I had transgressed the law enjoining upon us respect for our neighbour's property, I suffered every Saturday, for quite a number of minutes, considerable anxiety concerning my spiritual welfare. I filled that cap with gravel; I shied it up into trees—whence it had to be knocked down with stones like fruit before it is ripe; I converted it into a duster to rub out the faces I had chalked on the blackboard; I threw it down trap-doors into inaccessible cellars, and when, after school was over, the ingenious Fontanet succeeded in discovering it, it was nothing more than a miserable rag.

But a fairy watched over its destiny, for, when
Fontanet reappeared with it next day, it presented
most unexpectedly a clean, neat, almost elegant
appearance, and that not once, but always. The
fairy was Fontanet's elder sister, and this alone
constituted her a qualified housewife.

On more than one occasion, as I knelt at the
foot of the sacred tribunal, Fontanet's cap lay
whelmed at the bottom of the pool in the Great
Quadrangle, wherein I had flung it. At such
moments there was something peculiarly delicate
in my position.

What sentiment, you ask, impelled me so to
maltreat this cap? It was vengeance!

Fontanet used to tease me about a queer, old-
fashioned-looking satchel with which my uncle—
careful man—had presented me, to my undoing.
The satchel was much too large for me, and I was
much too small for the satchel. Moreover, the
satchel did not look like a satchel, the reason being
that it wasn't a satchel at all! It was an old
portfolio, which you could pull in and out like a
concertina; and my uncle's bootmaker had put a
strap to it.

This portfolio I held in cordial detestation, and
not without cause; but I cannot now say that I
think it was ugly enough to deserve all the in-
dignities that were heaped upon it. It was made

of red morocco, and adorned with a broad gold
tooling ; and surmounting its brass keyhole were a
crown and a coat of arms much worn and scratched.
It was lined with faded silk that had once been
blue. How I should delight to examine it if it still
survived. For, when I recollect the crown, I feel
sure that it must have been a royal crown, and as
the crest consisted—unless I dreamt it—of three
fleurs-de-lys half obliterated with a penknife, I
now suspect that this same portfolio originally
belonged to a Minister of Louis XVI.

But Fontanet, who didn't stop to consider the
thing in its antiquarian aspect, could never see me
with it on my back but he must bombard it with
snowballs in winter, chestnuts in autumn, and
india-rubber balls all the year round.

In point of fact, my schoolfellows—and Fontanet
himself—had only one fault to find with my satchel,
and that was, that it was out of the common ; it
was not as other satchels were. Hence all the woes
that it brought upon me. Children have a posi-
tively brutal reverence for convention. They will
put up with nothing distinctive or original. This
characteristic my uncle had not sufficiently borne in
mind when he bestowed on me that most pernicious
present. Fontanet's satchel was a hideous thing.
Both his elder brothers had dragged and battered it
about on the Lycée forms before him, and it could

not have presented a more disreputable appearance.
The leather was all scratched and cracked, the
straps had gone and had been replaced by string;
but as there was nothing unique about it, as it was
a satchel, Fontanet got off scot-free. No sooner,
however, did I make my appearance in the play-
ground with my portfolio on my back, than I was
greeted with ear-splitting yells, surrounded, set
upon, and laid flat upon my belly. Fontanet called it
making me play turtle, and he would get up and
sit straddle-legged upon my back. He was not
heavy, but oh! the humiliation of the thing! As
soon as I was on my feet again, I promptly jumped
on his cap!

Alas! his cap was ever new, and my preposterous
satchel indestructible. Our mutual outrages were
linked together by inexorable fate, even as the long
tale of tragedies that befel the ancient House of
Atreus.

IX

THE LAST WORDS OF DECIUS MUS

THIS morning, as I was strolling along the quays, rummaging among the bookstalls, I happened to come across an odd volume of Livy in the penny box. As I stood idly turning the pages, I chanced upon the following passage: "The remnants of the Roman army made their way to Canusium under cover of night," and this sentence reminded me of Monsieur Chotard. Now, when my thoughts light upon Monsieur Chotard, they do not leave him in a hurry; and I was still thinking of him as I went in for lunch. A smile still played about my mouth, and I was called upon to reveal the reason.

"The reason, my children," said I; "the reason is none other than Monsieur Chotard."

"And who is Chotard, pray, that he causes you this amusement?" they inquired.

"I will tell you," said I. "If I bore you, well, at all events, pretend to be listening, and don't let me suspect that I am an irrepressible babbler, babbling stories to himself.

"I was fourteen, and I was in the Third. My professor's name was Chotard. He had the florid complexion of an old monk, and an old monk he was!

"Brother Chotard had been one of the most docile members of the flock of Saint Francis when, in 1830, he flung his monkish habit to the winds and donned the raiment of the layman, which, however, he never succeeded in wearing to advantage. Wherefore did Brother Chotard take this step? Some say it was love, others that it was fear, and that after those three Glorious Days in July, the Sovereign People having hurled a good few cabbage-stalks at the Capuchin of ———, Brother Chotard leapt over the monastery walls in order to preserve his persecutors from committing so heinous a sin as maltreating a friar.

"The good brother was a man of parts. He took his degree, began to teach, and lived so long and so well, that his hair was going grey, his cheeks growing fat, and his nose turning red, when I and my comrades found ourselves placed beneath his ferule.

"What a bellicose professor he was! You ought to have seen him when, book in hand, he marched the army of Brutus to Philippi. What courage!

What nobility of soul! What heroism! But he chose his own time to be a hero, and that time was not the present time. In real life Monsieur Chotard was an obviously anxious and timid man. He was easily frightened.

"He was afraid of thieves, he was afraid of dogs, he was afraid of thunder, he was afraid of carts, and, indeed, of anything from which the hide of an honest man could possibly sustain an injury, whether from far or near.

"True, it was only his body that dwelt among us; his spirit was away in the dim and distant Past. He fought and died, this worthiest of men, with Leonidas at Thermopylæ. He navigated the waters of Salamis on the ship of Themistocles. He fought at Cannæ side by side with Paulus Æmilius. He fell, bathed in gore, into Lake Trasimenus, and, many years after, a fisherman plying his nets in those waters brought to the surface the ring he had worn as a Roman knight. At Pharsalia, he breathed defiance against Cæsar and the gods themselves. He brandished his shattered brand over the dead body of Varus in the forest of Hercynia. He was a famous warrior! But notwithstanding his resolve to sell his life dearly on the banks of the Aegospotamos, notwithstanding his proud determination to drain the cup of freedom and death in beleagured Numantia,

Monsieur Chotard was by no means above plotting with crafty captains and lending himself to the most perfidious of stratagems.

" One of the stratagems which called for special mention was that which Monsieur Chotard described when commenting on a passage in Ælian whereby the hostile army is lured into a narrow gorge, and crushed beneath huge masses of rock.

" He did not go on to tell us whet' er the hostile forces frequently obliged by lending themselves to this engaging manœuvre. But let me come to the idiosyncrasy by which Monsieur Chotard particularly impressed himself on the minds of his pupils.

" Whenever he gave us a composition to write— Latin or French—it was always about battles, sieges, expiatory and propitiatory ceremonies, and it was when he came to give out the corrected versions of these narratives that he brought his finest eloquence into play. Whether in French or Latin, his language and delivery were always expressive of the same warlike enthusiasm. He sometimes had to interrupt the flow of his ideas in order to administer some well-merited rebukes to his class, but the tone of his discourse remained heroic, even when he was occupied with such inglorious matters as these. And so it fell out that, speaking, now like a consul exhorting his troops, now like a third-form master distributing ' impots,' but always in the same grandiose tone of voice, he greatly bewildered his pupils; it being quite impossible to tell whether the schoolmaster or the consul was speaking. One day he completely surpassed himself in this line, and delivered a really incomparable oration. We all got this speech up by heart, and I took care to write it down in my notebook without omitting a word of it.

"Here it is as I heard it, and as I hear it now, for the voice of the unctuous Chotard still resounds in my ears, filling them with its solemn and majestic monotone:

"'THE LAST WORDS OF DECIUS MUS

"' Prepared to offer his life as a sacrifice to the Deities of the other world, just ere he drove his spurs into the flanks of his impetuous courser, Decius Mus turned a last time to his comrades in arms, saying ':

"Unless you keep silence better than this, I shall keep the whole class in. 'For my country's sake I am about to enter into immortality. The abyss awaits me. I am about to lay down my life for the common weal.' Fontanet, you will copy out ten pages of rudiment. 'Thus, in his wisdom, hath ordained Jupiter Capitolinus, eternal guardian of the Eternal City.' Nozière, if, as I believe, you are passing on your work to Fontanet for him to copy,

as he usually does, I shall write to your father.
'It is meet and right for a citizen to lay down his
life for the common weal. Envy me, therefore,
and weep not for me.' It is silly to laugh at nothing, Nozière; you will stay in on Thursday. 'My
example will dwell among you.' This giggling
is more than I can put up with; I shall inform the
Principal of your conduct. 'And I shall behold,
as I look forth from Elysium, where the shades of
Heroes abide, the Virgins of the Republic laying
chaplets of flowers at the foot of my statues!'"

"In those days I possessed a prodigious faculty
for laughing. I employed it to the full on The
Last Words of Decius Mus; and when, after
supplying us with this most potent reason for mirth,
Monsieur Chotard proceeded to remark that it
was inept to laugh at nothing, I buried my face in
a dictionary and became dead to the world. Those
who, when they were boys of fifteen, were never
doubled up with laughter what time the 'impots'
descended upon them like hailstones, have missed
one of the luxuries of life.

"But it must not be supposed that my capa-
bilities were limited to playing the fool in class. I
was a good enough little Humanist in my way,
very keenly alive to all that is attractive and noble
in what we so happily call Belles Lettres.

"I had, even in those days, a great love of style both in Latin and French, a love which I still retain, despite the advice and example of many of my more successful contemporaries. As usually happens in the case of people whose cherished convictions are regarded with scant esteem, I have gloried in what is perhaps but a vain and foolish thing after all. I have kept my faith in Literature, and I am still a staunch upholder of the Classics. Call me an aristocrat, call me a mandarin if you will, I still believe that six or seven years of literary culture will impart to the mind, duly prepared to receive it, a loftiness, a strength, an elegance and a beauty, attainable by no other means.

"For myself, Sophocles and Virgil have afforded me moments of pure delight. Monsieur Chotard, yes, Monsieur Chotard, with the aid of Titus Livius, inspired me with noble dreams! The imagination of children is a wondrous thing; and splendid are the visions that fill the little rascals' heads. When he did not send me off into fits of laughter, Monsieur Chotard used to inspire me with enthusiasm.

"Every time I heard him, with his unctuous pulpit tones, slowly declaiming that sentence: 'The remnants of the Roman army made their way to Canusium under cover of night,' I beheld a silent host pass by in the bare, moonlit country, along a road fringed with tombs, their ashen faces smeared with blood and dust, their helmets dented, their breastplates battered and tarnished, their swords shattered at the hilt. And this ghost-like procession, as it melted slowly into the night, was so grave, so mournful, and so majestic, that my heart leapt within me for grief and admiration."

X

THE HUMANITIES

I WILL tell you what I am reminded of every year by the stormy skies of autumn, the first lamp-lit dinners, the leaves turning yellow on the shivering trees. I will tell you what I see when I cross the Luxembourg Gardens in the early days of October, when a vague hint of sadness makes them lovelier than ever: for it is the time when the leaves fall one by one upon the white shoulders of the statues. What I behold at such times in these gardens is just a little fellow trotting along on his way to school with his hands in his pockets and his satchel slung over his shoulder, hopping about merry as a sparrow. It is only my inward eye that beholds him, for this little fellow is a ghost, the ghost of that which was *I* five-and-twenty years ago. When he existed I thought but little about him, but now that he is no more I have taken a great fancy to him. On the whole he was better worth loving than all the other "I's" that I have lost since then. He was thoughtless, very thoughtless; but his heart was gentle, and I will do him the justice to say that he has not bequeathed to me a single unwelcome memory. It is a little one that I have lost, and, natural enough it is that I should feel his loss, natural enough that I should see him again in my thoughts and take pleasure in dwelling on his memory.

Five-and-twenty years ago, at this same season, he was trotting along to school across these beautiful gardens. His heart was the least bit heavy, for the holidays were over.

However, on he jogged with his books on his back and his top in his pocket. The thought of seeing his school-fellows again soon restored his spirits. There would be so much to tell, so much to hear. Hadn't he got to ask Laboriette whether he had really been out shooting in the *Forêt de l'Aigle*, and hadn't he got to tell him how he himself had ridden on horseback among the mountains of Auvergne? Such an achievement as that is not the sort of thing you keep to yourself. And then, how jolly to see the other fellows again! How he longed to set eyes on Fontanet, his chum, who quizzed him so good-humouredly—Fontanet, who was about as big as a rat, and as resourceful as Ulysses, and who took the lead in everything with a sort of natural grace. He felt quite light-hearted at the thought of seeing Fontanet again.

Such was his state of mind as he made his way across the Luxembourg in the cool morning air. All that he saw then, I still behold to-day. The same heaven and the same earth. Everything has a soul, as it used to have of old, a soul which brings joy or melancholy or misgiving to my heart; only the little boy is no more.

Thus it is that the older I become the more interest I take in the children going back to school. Had I been a boarder in a Lycée, my school-day memories would have been a horror, and I should banish them from my mind; but my parents did not consign me to such a prison. I went as a day-boy to a somewhat cloistral and sequestered old college, and every day I saw the streets, every day I saw my home. I was not cut off as boarders are from world and home alike. I had no sense of thraldom or constraint, my ideas expanded with that sweetness and strength which Freedom bestows on everything that comes to maturity within her pale. Hatred had no place in my thoughts. If I was inquisitive and eager to know the ins and outs of things, it was that I might love them the better. Everything I saw as I went my way along the street—men, animals, and things—helped me more than one would believe to feel and appreciate the simple fundamental elements of life.

There is nothing like a street to make a boy

understand the working of the social machine.
Let him see the milk-women, the water-carriers,
and coalmen on their morning rounds; let him
take stock of the grocers', the butchers', and the
wine merchants' shops; let him see a regiment of
soldiers pass down the street with its band playing;
let him, in a word, sniff in the air of the street,
and he will feel that the law of labour is a divine
law, and that everyone must perform his appointed
task in this world of ours.

I owe it to these morning and evening walks
from home to school, and from school back home
again, that I still retain an affectionate curiosity
regarding shop-people and their trades. I must
confess, however, that I liked some better than
others. The stationers who exhibited illustrated
story-books in their windows were my earliest
favourites, and times without number have I stood
flattening my nose against their windows reading
those pictured legends through from beginning
to end.

I read numbers of them in no time. Some of
them were of the fanciful order. They set my
imagination to work, and helped to develop that
seeing faculty without which, even in the realm
of the exact sciences, no discovery is made. Some
of them told plain and thrilling tales of what
people did and suffered, and these brought me for

the first time to contemplate the most terrible thing there is—or, rather, the one terrible thing —Fate. Ah! yes, I owe a deal to those coloured sheets they print at Épinal.

But later on, when I was fourteen or fifteen, I gave up looking in the grocers' shops, though I confess that their boxes of candied fruits long continued to excite my admiration. I turned up my nose at the drapers' shops, and gave up trying to discover the significance of the mysterious gilt Y upon their shop signs. I scarcely troubled myself to unravel the childish rebuses worked into the wrought metal grilles of the ancient wineshops, where a quince or a comet figured in hammered iron.

My tastes had grown more fastidious, and the only wares in which I took an interest were prints, curios, and old books.

Ye old rapacious Jews of the *Rue du Cherche Midi*, ye artless book vendors of the quays, my masters all! How greatly am I beholden to you! To you I owe as much, nay, even more than to the University itself, for the training of my intellect. It was you, good folk, who displayed to my enchanted gaze the mysterious tokens of a bygone age and all manner of precious memorials of the pilgrimage of the human mind. Even as I turned over the old tomes in your boxes, or gazed within your dusty stalls laden with the sad relics of our

sires and their golden thoughts, I became insensibly
imbued with the most wholesome of philosophies.
Yes, my friends, it was when rummaging about
among those musty books, those scraps of tarnished
metal-work, those fragments of old, worm-eaten
carvings which you used to barter for your daily
bread, that my childish spirit recognised how frail
and fleeting are all the things of this world. I
divined that we living beings were but ever-changing
figures in the world's great Shadow Show; and even
then my heart inclined to sadness, gentleness, and
pity.

Thus, the open-air school taught me many a
lofty lesson; but the home school was more
profitable still. The family board, with its fair
white cloth, its clear, sparkling decanters, the
tranquil faces, the easy, natural talk—from all
these things a boy may learn to love and to understand the lowly and hallowed elements of human
life. If he is fortunate enough to have, as I had,
kindly and intelligent parents, the table-talk to
which he listens will give balance to his mind, and
dispose his heart to love. Day by day he eats of
that Blessed Bread which the Master brake and gave
unto the pilgrims in the inn at Emmaus, and he
murmurs even as they, "Doth not my heart burn
within me."

Meals taken in boarding-school refectories have

not this sweetness and this grace. Ah! Home is a famous school!

However, I should be grievously misunderstood were it supposed that I wish to underrate classical culture: I believe indeed that there is nothing so valuable in shaping the mind as the study of classical antiquity, carried out according to the methods of the old French Humanists. By " Humanities," we mean grace, elegance; and it is a word we may fittingly apply to classical culture.

The little fellow of whom I was speaking just now with a warmth of sympathy that may perhaps be forgiven me—he is but a ghost, after all—this little fellow that used to wend his way to school across the Luxembourg Gardens as merry as a young sparrow, was, believe me, no indifferent Humanist. Little boy though he was, he could feel and appreciate the strength and majesty of Old Rome, the splendours of the poetry of Antiquity. For all that he was a day-boy, for all that he was free to wander at will among the bookstalls and to dine at home with his father and mother, he was by no means insensible to the lordly rhetoric of the schools. Far from that, he was just as "Attic," just as thorough-going a Ciceronian as you could expect to find in a troop of urchins under the governance of a few well-meaning old dominies.

He strove but little for glory, and his name was rarely blazoned on the prize-lists; but he toiled hard in order to "amuse himself," as La Fontaine's saying goes. His versions were very well turned, his Latin speeches would have deserved the encomiums of Monsieur l'Inspecteur himself had they not generally been marred by some careless blunder. Have I not said Livy wrung from him tears of generous sympathy!

But it was when he set foot on the shores of Hellas that he first knew what Beauty was in its superb simplicity. It was a tardy arrival. Early in his career his spirit had been saddened by Æsop's fables. His first Greek professor had a crooked back—a crooked back and a crooked mind. Perhaps you picture to yourself Thersites conducting the young Galatians into the groves of the Muses. That was not how it struck the pupil. You might perhaps imagine that as his humpbacked professor specialised as an exponent of Æsop, he might have been suitably employed on such a task. Not a bit of it! He was a spurious hunchback—a great hulking hunchback—devoid of wit, devoid of kindness; disposed to evil; the most unjust of men. He was good for nothing, not even for telling you what a hunchback thinks of things. Moreover, those dry little fables, which bear the name of Æsop, have come down to us clipped and pared by some Byzantine monk who must have carried a cramped and sterile brain beneath his tonsure. I knew nothing and cared little about their origin in those days; but the opinion I had of them I still retain.

After Æsop they gave us Homer. I saw Thetis rising like a white cloud from the sea; I saw Nausicaa and her maidens, the palm-tree of Delos, and the sky and the land and the sea; and I saw Andromache smiling through her tears. . . . I understood — I felt it all. For six months I was lost in the Odyssey. It earned me many punishments; but what cared I for "impots"? I was sailing with Ulysses over the wine-dark sea. Next came the tragic poets. Of Æschylus I could make but little. But Sophocles, Euripides! They opened the gates of an enchanted world to me, a world of heroes and heroines. From them I learned the poetry of calamity. At every fresh tragedy I read I was a prey to new thrills, new griefs, new shudders.

To the Alcestis and the Antigone I owe the noblest dreams that ever schoolboy was visited by. As I sat at my ink-stained desk, my head buried in my dictionary, forms of godlike beauty passed before my vision; I beheld arms of gleaming ivory falling upon snowy tunics; I heard voices sweeter than the sweetest melody mourning most musically.

This, again, brought down fresh punishments upon
me. But I deserved them all! I was "occupying
myself with matters extraneous to the work of the
class." Alas! the habit has clung to me. In
whatever class in life's school they put me for the
rest of my days, I am afraid that, old man though
I be, I shall still incur the rebukes I received as
a boy at the hands of my professor: "Monsieur
Pierre Nozière, your mind is occupied with matters
extraneous to the work of the class!"

But it was, above all, of a winter's evening, when
I escaped into the streets again after school was
done, that I revelled in this visionary glow, these
soundless harmonies. I halted beneath lamp-posts ;
I stayed my steps by flaring shop-windows to con a
line or two, and then recited them in an undertone
as I pursued my way. The streets—the narrow
streets of the faubourg—on which the shadows of
night were beginning to fall, would then be filled
with the bustle of a busy winter's eve. Often
enough I collided with a pastry-cook's boy with
his hamper on his head, dreaming his dreams as
I was dreaming mine ; or else I would suddenly
feel on my cheek the hot breath of some unlucky
horse tugging at his load. Nor did reality mar
the beauty of my dreams, because I loved those
dear old streets of mine, whose every stone had
seen me growing into manhood. One evening I

read some lines of the Antigone by the lantern of a vendor of baked chestnuts, and even now, after a quarter of a century, I can never think of the line that begins :

"O tomb ! O bridal bed !"

without seeing the man of Auvergne blowing into a paper bag, or feeling my side grow warm with the heat of the stove where his chestnuts were a-roasting. And the memory of this worthy blended harmoniously in my mind with the lament of the Theban maid.

This was how I learned a deal of poetry; this was how I made many a useful and valuable acquaintance ; this was how I put the finishing touch on my humanities. It was a method that answered well in my case. It might fail utterly in another's. I should take great care not to recommend it to anybody else.

All the same, I have to confess that, nurtured as I had been on Homer and Sophocles, I was " lacking in taste" when I took up my rhetoric. My professor of rhetoric it was who told me so, and I am quite ready to believe him. The taste one has, or the taste one displays, at seventeen is seldom good. To bring about an improvement in my own, my rhetoric professor advised me to make a careful study of the entire writings of Casimir Delavigne. I did not follow his advice. Sophocles had given a certain bent to my mind, and that bent was not to be got rid of. I did not then, and do not now, regard my professor of rhetoric as one gifted with a discriminating taste in literary matters; but though he had a surly temper, he disdained meanness, and his conduct was as straight as a die. His views on literature may have been a trifle heterodox; but, at any rate, he showed us by his own example how an upright man should act.

It was a science that had its reward, for Monsieur Charron was respected by all his pupils. Children never err in their estimate of the moral worth of their instructors. The opinions I held twenty-five years ago of the abusive hunchback and the worthy Charron I still retain to-day.

But the shades of evening are descending upon the plane-trees in the Luxembourg, and the little ghost whose presence I evoked grows faint and more faint amid the gathering gloom. Farewell, then, little ego—little " me "—that I have lost Never should I cease to mourn for you had you not come back to me, and with an added beauty, in my son.

XI

THE GROVE OF MYRTLE

I

A S a child I had shown great intelligence, but when I was about seventeen I grew stupid. I used to be
so nervous in those days, that I could
not make my bow or take my seat
in company without my forehead becoming moist
with perspiration. The presence of women sent
me off into a panic. I observed—at least in the
letter—the precept from the *Imitation of Christ*
which I had learned in some junior class or other,
and which I had remembered because the version,
which is Corneille's, had struck me as quaint :

> "Fuis avec un grand soin la pratique des femmes ;
> Ton ennemi par là peut savoir ton défaut.
> Recommande en commun aux bontés du Très-Haut
> Celles dont les vertus embellissent les âmes,
> Et, sans en voir jamais qu'avec un prompt adieu
> Aime les toutes, mais en Dieu." [1]

---

[1] "Take heed that thou flee the company of women ;
By that road thy enemy may find thee vulnerable.
Commend to the mercies of the Most High, in general,

L

I followed the advice of the old monk and
mystic ; I followed it, but very much against the
grain ; I should have preferred a less prompt adieu.

Among my mother's friends there was one
woman in whose society I should have particularly
delighted to linger, with whom I should have loved
to have long talks. She was the wife of a distin-
guished pianist, Adolphe Gance, who had been cut off
at an early age. Her name was Alice, and though
I had never really seen her hair, her eyes, her teeth,
for how can one see what is but a brilliant, sparkling,
dazzling vision, to me she seemed fairer than a dream,
dowered with more than mortal loveliness. My
mother used to say that, taken separately, there was
nothing out of the common about any of Madame
Gance's features. Every time my mother expressed
this view, my father shook his head incredulously.
Doubtless he, good man, did as I did, and refrained
from taking Madame Gance's features separately.
And, whatever the details were like, the general
effect was charming. But never heed what my
mother said ; Madame Gance was beautiful, I give
you my word for it. Madame Gance attracted me :

All those whose souls are adorned by virtues,
And, never seeing them save to bid them a swift God-speed,
Love them all, but in the Lord."

A rather verbose expansion of the precept in the *Imitation :*
" Be not thou too familiar with any one woman, but commend
all good women generally to God."

beauty is so sweet and kind! Madame Gance made me afraid : beauty is an awesome thing!

One evening my father was entertaining a few friends, and Madame Gance came into the room with a good-natured look upon her face that encouraged me a little. Sometimes, with men, she would assume an air of leisurely condescension as of one tossing bread crumbs to the sparrows. Then, without any warning, she would put on a lofty manner of icy hauteur, and move her fan to and fro with a weary, bored expression on her countenance. I never knew how to account for this. I can thoroughly account for it now : Madame Gance was a coquette. That is the whole of the matter.

But, as I was saying, when Madame Gance came into the drawing-room that night she tossed every one, even the humblest—and that was I—a crumb, so to speak, of her benevolence. I never took my eyes off her, and as I gazed I thought I detected a shade of melancholy in her expression. I was quite overcome, being, you see, a soft-hearted creature. She was asked to play something, and she gave us one of Chopin's Nocturnes. I have never heard anything so beautiful. It seemed as though her very fingers, her white, shapely fingers, from which she had just removed her rings, were lightly touching my ears with the most heavenly of caresses. When she had finished playing, I went to her instinctively, and, hardly knowing what I was doing, escorted her to her seat, and then sat down beside her. As I breathed in the fragrance that exhaled from her bosom, I shut my eyes. She asked me if I was fond of music; her voice sent a thrill through me. I opened my eyes again, and I saw that she was looking at me. That look was my undoing.

"Yes, sir," I answered in confusion.

Since the earth did not open and swallow me up, it is clear that Nature is indifferent to the most fervent supplications of mortal men.

Up in my bedroom that night, I did nothing but call myself an idiot and a boor. When morning came I pondered long and deeply on the matter; but, no, I could discover no extenuating circumstance. "You want to tell a woman she is beautiful—all too beautiful—and that she can make the piano sigh and sob, and all you do is just to blurt out two preposterous words: 'Yes, sir.' To be so destitute of the power of expression as that is just a little bit too much of a good thing. Pierre Nozière, you are a fool, an imbecile! Go and hide yourself!" Unfortunately, I couldn't even do that properly. I had to put in an appearance at school, at table, and in the street. With the fellows at school I could at least have exchanged fisticuffs if I had liked, and there is some sort of dignity about doing that. But with my mother's

women friends I was in most pitiable case. I
realised to the full the worth of the precept laid
down in the *Imitation* :

"Fuis avec un grand soin la pratique des femmes."

"What salutary advice," said I to myself.
"Had I shunned Madame Gance that fatal evening
when she played that Nocturne with such poetic
feeling, and made the air shudder with delight;
had I shunned her then, she would not have asked
me whether I was fond of music, and I should
never have answered, 'Yes, sir.'"

Those two words, "Yes, sir," were for ever ring-
ing in my ears. The recollection of them was
always with me, or, to speak more accurately, some
horrible psychical phenomenon made it seem as
though time had suddenly come to a standstill, and
that the dreadful moment that had been startled
by that irreparable utterance, "Yes, sir," was being
indefinitely prolonged. It was not remorse that
was torturing my soul. Remorse itself were sweet
compared with what I was feeling then. For six
weeks I remained in a condition of sombre melancholy, and after that my parents themselves realised
that I had lost my senses.

What put the coping-stone on my imbecility was
that my mind was as daring as my manners were
shy. As a general rule, the intellect in young

people is crude and undecided. Mine was rigid
and inflexible. I believed that I was in possession
of the truth. I was violent and revolutionary,
when I was alone. When I was alone, what a
blade, what a slashing fellow, I used to be! I have
changed a deal since then. Now, I am not over-
much in awe of my contemporaries. I try to make
myself as snug as possible between those who have
more brains than I and those who have less; and
I trust to the cleverness of the former. On the
other hand, I am not without misgivings when I
come to look myself in the face. . . . But I was
telling you about something that happened to me
when I was seventeen. You will readily imagine
that such a blend of shyness and audacity made me
cut a most ridiculous figure.

Six months after the frightful occurrence I have
just related to you, I, having finished my course
of rhetoric with some credit to myself, was sent by
my father for a holiday in the country. He gave
me a letter to one of the humblest and worthiest of
his colleagues, an old country doctor who was in
practice at Saint Patrice, and thither I went. Saint
Patrice is a little village on the coast of Normandy.
Behind it is a forest, and on the seaward side it
slopes gently down towards a sandy beach hemmed
in between two cliffs. At the time of which I am
speaking this beach was wild and lonely. The sea,

which I then beheld for the first time ; and the woods, whose peace was so healing, so benign, sent me into ecstasies. The dim expanse of woods and waters harmonised with the vague promptings of my soul. I went for rides in the forest ; I rolled half naked on the strand, filled with a longing for something—I knew not what—which seemed always at hand, yet was to be found nowhere.

All day long I was alone ; and my tears would flow without cause. Sometimes, indeed, my heart grew so full that I thought I should die. In a word, I was ill at ease ; but is there in the whole world anything to compare with the restlessness that then possessed me ? No ! I call those woods, whose branches whipped my face as I brushed through them—I call those woods to witness—those cliffs, whose heights I scaled to watch the sun sinking in the sea—those cliffs will bear me out—there is nought to compare with the malady which then tormented me, nought to compare with a young man's early dreams. If desire lends a grace to whatsoever be the object of it, then the desire of the unknown makes beautiful the Universe.

Shrewd enough as I am, I have always been curiously unsophisticated in some things. I should, perhaps, have gone many a day without discovering the cause of my unrest and vague longings, had not a poet revealed the mystery to me.

Even in my school-days I conceived an affection for the poets, an affection which, happily, I have ever since retained. As a boy of seventeen I adored Virgil, and I understood him almost as well as if my professors had never expounded his meaning to me. During my holidays I always carried a Virgil in my pocket. It was a little, cheap English edition, and I have it still. I cherish it as tenderly as it is possible for me to cherish anything   Withered flowers fall from its pages every time I open it. Those that have been there the longest are the flowers that I gathered in the woods of Saint Patrice, where I was so happily unhappy when a boy of seventeen.

One day when I was wandering on the skirts of this wood, breathing in with delight the fragrance of the new-mown hay, while the wind, blowing in softly from the sea, brought the savour of salt to my lips, I was seized with an unconquerable sensation of weariness. I sat down on the ground, and remained for a long time gazing at the clouds floating by in the heavens. Then, by force of habit, I opened my Virgil and read : *Hic quos durus amor* . . .

"Here shy glades conceal those whom unrelenting love hath with cruel venom consumed in lingering death, and all around them groves of myrtle cast their shade."

"And the groves of myrtle cast their shade. . . ." Oh! I knew it! I knew that grove of myrtle.

But I knew not its name. Virgil had just revealed to me the cause of my malady. Thanks to him, I knew that it was Love.

But, as yet, I knew not whom I loved. That, it was given to me to discover the following winter, when I saw Madame Gance again.

Doubtless you are gifted with greater perspicacity than I possessed. You, of course, have long since divined that it was Alice whom I loved. Oh, wonderful irony! The woman I loved was the very woman in whose presence I had covered myself with ridicule, and who needs must have something worse than a sorry opinion of me. Here was matter for despair. But despair was not in vogue. Our sires had made too free with it and worn it threadbare. I did nothing sublime or terrible. I did not seek the seclusion of some mouldering cloister. I did not wander disconsolate amid the waste places of the earth. I cried not to the Northern blasts. I merely went on being miserable —and I took my degree.

Even the modicum of happiness that was vouchsafed me contained a sting ; for it consisted in seeing Alice, in hearing her voice, and saying to myself, " She is the one woman in the world whom I can love, I am the one man in the world she cannot endure." When she played the piano, I used to take my stand beside her to turn over the music, and watch the play of the little wavelets of hair upon her white neck. But, in order that I might run no risk of blurting out another " Yes, sir," I vowed that I would speak to her no more. Before long I had to make a change in my way of life, and I lost sight of Alice without having broken my vow.

II

I discovered Madame Gance again at a watering-place in the mountains this very summer. Fifty years have left their mark upon that lovely face, the face to which I owe my first and most delicious experience of love's unrest.

Her features, on which Time has left his trace, are fair and gracious still, and I deemed that, being now a grey-haired man, I might renounce that boyish vow of mine. Approaching her, therefore, I made my bow and said, "How do you do, Madame Gance."

Alas ! the eager emotion of my youth had fled, my voice was steady, my countenance composed.

She recognised me pretty readily. Our memories formed a link between us. We used to have long talks together about old times, and did our utmost to help each other to beguile the somewhat unin-spiring round of hotel existence.

Before long, we discovered new subjects of

interest, new links of only too enduring a character. Our ailments and our vexations formed the staple of our conversation. All the morning we used to sit out in the sun on a green garden-seat discussing our rheumatism and our other trials and troubles. It was a topic not easily exhausted. Sometimes, by way of relief, we would mingle the past with the present.

"How very beautiful you were, madame," I remarked to her one day; "and how people used to rave about you."

"Yes," she answered with a smile, "I can acquiesce in that without impropriety, for I am an old woman now. Yes," she went on, "I was thought a good deal of, and the recollection of it brings a solace to my growing years. I have had some handsome compliments bestowed upon me; but I should perhaps surprise you if I told you which, of all the compliments that were ever paid me, is the one that touched me the most."

"Pray, tell me, I should so much like to know."

"Well, then, I will. One evening (it is a long time ago, now), a little bashful schoolboy became so dreadfully flurried as he looked at me, that he answered 'Yes, sir,' to a question I asked him. Never did I receive a token of admiration that flattered me so much, or pleased me more than that 'Yes, sir,' and the tone in which it was uttered!"

XII

THE SHADOW

I WAS in my twentieth year when an extraordinary thing happened to me. My father had sent me down into Lower Maine to see to a piece of family business, and I set out one afternoon from the pretty little town of Ernée on a twenty-mile ride. I was making for the district of Saint Jean in order to pay a visit to the house—at that time untenanted—which had sheltered my father's family for more than two hundred years. It was early in December. Snow had been falling since morning, and the road, which lay between two quickset hedges, had given way in many places, so that my horse and I had much ado to avoid the quagmires.

But, when I got to within five or six miles of Saint Jean, the surface began to improve, and, despite the fact that a furious gale had sprung up, and that the frozen snow was whipping my face, I put my horse to the gallop. The trees which lined the road flew past me in the darkness, like hideous, stricken ghosts. How horrible they were, those trees, lopped off at the top, covered with lumps and gashes, extending frightful, twisted limbs. They awoke a kind of terror in me, for I could not help letting my mind run on a story which a *vicaire* at Saint-Marcel d'Ernée had told me the night before. One of these trees—one of those mutilated veterans of Le Bocage — a chestnut that had been decapitated more than two hundred years ago, and was as hollow as a tower, was riven from top to bottom by lightning on the 24th of February 1849. Looking through the fissure, some people saw the skeleton of a man standing bolt upright within it, with a gun in one hand and a rosary in the other. On a watch, which was picked up at his feet, was engraved the name of Claude Nozière. This Claude—my father's great-uncle—had been a great smuggler in his day. In 1794 he attached himself to the Chouans, and joined the band commanded by Treton, commonly called Jambe d'Argent. Sorely wounded and hotly pursued by the partisans of the Republic, the hunted man went to hide himself, and to die, in the hollow of this old chestnut. Friend and foe alike were ignorant of the fate that had befallen him ; and it was not until fifty years after his death that the mystery was solved, and the old Chouan's grave laid bare by a stroke of lightning.

His story came into my mind as the leafless, stunted trees flew past, and I put spurs to my horse. It was pitch dark when I reached Saint Jean.

Swaying to and fro in the wind, the signboard creaked drearily on its chains in the darkness as I made my way up to the inn. Having attended to my horse myself, I entered the parlour and threw myself into an old arm-chair which stood in the chimney corner. As I sat warming myself, the firelight shone upon the countenance of my hostess. She was old and hideously ugly. Her features seemed prematurely covered with the dust of the grave, and all that was discernible in her face was a nose half eaten away and a pair of red-rimmed, expressionless orbs. I was a stranger, and she kept darting furtive and mistrustful glances in my direction. To set her mind at rest, I told her my name was Nozière—a name I felt sure she would know. But she only shook her head, and replied that there were no Nozières left. However, she consented to prepare me some supper, and, throwing a faggot on the hearth, she quitted the room.

I was weary and low-spirited, weighed down with an indescribable sensation of mental oppression.

Thick-coming fancies, scenes of violence and gloom, tormented my imagination. After a while, I fell into a fitful doze ; but in my uneasy slumber

I could hear the moaning of the wind in the chimney, and now and again a gust of more than usual violence would fling the ashes from the hearth over my very boots.

When, a few minutes afterwards, I opened my eyes, I beheld a sight that I shall never forget. I saw at the far end of the room, silhouetted with the utmost distinctness against the whitewashed wall, a motionless shadow—the shadow of a young girl. The form was so instinct with gentleness, purity, and charm, that, as I beheld it, I felt all my weariness, all my melancholy, melt away into wonder and delight.

I gazed at this vision for what, I suppose, was about a minute—it may have been more, it may have been less; for I have no means of measuring the exact length of time. Then I turned round to see who it could be that was casting so lovely a shadow. Not a soul was in the room . . . no one but the old woman spreading a white cloth on the table. Again I looked at the wall : the shadow had disappeared.

Then something resembling a lover's longing took possession of my heart, and I grieved for the loss I had just sustained.

My mind was perfectly rational, and I pondered for a few seconds on what had occurred. Then, turning to the landlady, I said :

"Mother, tell me, who was it that was standing there a second or two ago?"

The old woman answered in a tone of surprise that she had seen no one.

I hastened to the door. Snow was falling heavily; it lay thick and white upon the ground, yet not a footprint was to be seen.

"Mother, are you sure that there is not a woman in the house?"

The old woman replied that she was quite alone in the place.

I next endeavoured to ascertain, by careful observation, the precise position that a person would have had to occupy to cast a shadow where I saw it. I pointed to this spot with my hand, and said:

"There, that is where she was, I tell you."

The hag approached with a taper in her hand, and, fixing her horrible expressionless eyes upon me, she exclaimed:

"Now I know that you are not deceiving me; I know that you are really a Nozière. Can you be a son of Jean Nozière, the one that is a doctor in Paris? I knew young René, an uncle of his. He, too, used to see a woman that no one else could see. No doubt it is a curse that God has laid upon the family for the sin committed by Claude, the Chouan, who went to perdition with the baker's wife."

" Do you mean the Claude whose skeleton was discovered in a hollow tree, holding a gun and a rosary ? " I asked.

" My good young sir, that rosary was no good to him. He had lost his soul for a woman."

The old woman had no more to tell me about the matter; but I could scarcely put my lips to the bread, the bacon and eggs, and cider that she placed before me. I was continually turning to look at the wall where I had seen the shadow. Oh! yes! I had seen it plainly enough. It was delicate, and more distinctly outlined than a shadow naturally produced by the flickering light of a fire or the smoky flame of a tallow candle.

Next day I went and looked at the deserted house where Claude and René had dwelt in their day. I scoured the neighbourhood; I cross-questioned the curé; but I learned nothing that would enable me to discover the identity of the young girl whose ghost I had seen.

Even now I am not so sure whether the old woman's account of the matter was the true one or not. Perhaps it was as she said ; perhaps there, in the bleak solitudes of Le Boçcage, some phantom had been wont to appear to those peasants whose descendant I am, and, maybe, it was the ancestral shadow which haunted of old my untutored, dreamy forefathers that presented itself with un-

M

wonted grace to the gaze of their visionary
child.

Was it indeed the Nozière family ghost that I saw
in the inn at Saint Jean, or was it not rather that a
sign was vouchsafed to me that winter's night—a
sign that the best that this life can bestow was to
be mine; that kindly Nature had granted me the
most precious of all her gifts—the gift of dreams?

THE BOOK OF SUZANNE

NOTE TO THE READER

THE reminiscences of Pierre Nozière come to an end with the story that we have just narrated, but we have thought it incumbent on us to add a few further pages by the same hand. The *Book of Suzanne* consists entirely of extracts from our friend's manuscripts, and in putting it together we have availed ourselves of such of Pierre Nozière's papers as have any connection, near or remote, with his daughter's childhood. We have thus been enabled to piece together a further chapter of this family record—a record which it was his intention to keep regularly written up, but which he only left in a fragmentary state.

SUZANNE

I

CHANTICLEER

ITHERTO Suzanne had not commenced her search for the beautiful ; but when she was fifteen weeks old, she set to work in real earnest.

It was in the dining-room. This dining-room presents a fallacious appearance of antiquity, because of the Faïence dishes, the stoneware bottles, the pewter flagons, and the phials of Venetian glass, with which the buffets are loaded. It is Suzanne's mamma who is responsible. She has arranged everything in the style of this new-fangled craze for curios. Amid all these antiquities, Suzanne, in her white embroidered frock, looks fresher and daintier than ever, and when you see her you say to yourself, " Well, here, at any rate, is a little creature that is absolutely new."

She is quite indifferent to all this ancient crockery, and to the dusky old portraits and great brass dishes that hang upon the walls. Later on, no doubt, these relics of the past will set all sorts of ideas running in her little head—fantastic, ridiculous, and charming. She will have her visions, and if she is of the imaginative cast of mind, she will employ her fancy on those matters of style and detail that lend such charm to life. I shall tell her all manner of whimsical tales, tales that will be no farther removed from the truth and infinitely more delightful than those they commonly call history. She will become madly in love with them. I should like everyone I love to have a touch of the motley. It gladdens the heart. Meanwhile, even the little Bacchus sitting astride his cask cannot cheat her of a smile. How serious we are at fifteen weeks.

The sky was a soft grey that morning. Some bindweed intertwined with the wild bryony engarlanded the casement with stars of divers hues. We had finished lunch, my wife and I, and we were chatting together after the fashion of people who have nothing particular to talk about. It was one of those hours when time glides onward like a tranquil river. You can almost see it flowing, and every word that is spoken seems like a little pebble cast into its waters. I rather think we were talking about the colour of Suzanne's eyes. It is an inexhaustible subject.

"They are slate blue. Yes."

"They have a tinge of old gold or onion broth. Yes."

"They have green lights in them. They have."

"It is all true! They are miracles of eyes!"

At this point, Suzanne came in. This time her eyes were the same colour as the sky—a most taking shade of grey.

She was carried in by her nursemaid.

To have been really in the fashion, it ought to have been a wet-nurse. But Suzanne, like La Fontaine's lamb—like all lambs, in fact—is suckled by her mother. I am perfectly well aware that if we play the rustic to this extent, we ought at least to study appearances and have a dry-nurse—a dry-nurse, with big pins and ribbons to her cap, just like a full-blown wet-nurse. She would have everything but the milk. But, then, the milk is merely for the baby; the ribbons and the pins are for the world. Mothers who are weak enough to suckle their children engage a dry-nurse to save their faces.

But Suzanne's mother is very thoughtless in these matters, and this attractive expedient never entered her mind.

Suzanne's nursemaid is a little peasant who, down in her own village, helped to bring up seven or eight little brothers. From morning till night she sings the songs of Lorraine. We let her have a day off to go and see Paris. She came back enchanted. She had seen some splendid radishes. The rest didn't strike her as being at all bad; but it was the radishes that won her fancy. She wrote home about them. Her native simplicity enables her to get on perfectly with Suzanne, who seems to have no eyes for anything in Nature but lamps and decanters.

When Suzanne appeared, hey presto! the dining-room was lit up with merriment. We laughed at Suzanne; Suzanne laughed at us. Folks that love each other can always make their meaning clear. Mamma stretched out her hands, and the sleeves of her dressing-gown fell back from her supple arms in the careless abandon that befits a warm summer morning. Then Suzanne held out her little arms, too, stiff in their starched piqué as a marionette's. She spread out her fingers, and five little pink rays peeped out from the bottom of her sleeves. Her mother, radiant with delight, took her tenderly on her knees, and the three of us were supremely happy, possibly because we were thinking about nothing. But this blissful state could not endure. Suzanne suddenly began to lean over towards the direction of the table, and opened her eyes so wide that they grew quite round, and she beat her arms about as though they had been made of wood, as, indeed, they appeared to be. There was a look of wonderment and admiration in her eyes. Into that touching stupidity of expression, the expression that babies have worn since the world began, there stole an indefinable gleam of Ariel-like intelligence.

Then she gave a sudden cry as of a stricken bird.

" Perhaps a pin has pricked her," said her mother, who was, happily, very much disposed to look on the practical side of things. " One never knows when those English pins are coming undone, and Suzanne has eight of them about her." But no ; it was not a pin that had pricked her ; it was her love of the Beautiful.

" Love of the Beautiful at fifteen weeks? Rubbish ! " you exclaim.

Well, then, judge for yourself.

Having nearly succeeded in worming herself out of her mother's arms, she was dabbing her little fists on the table, and tugging and pushing with might and main. With much puffing, spluttering, and babbling, she managed at length to seize hold of a plate. On the plate an old rustic craftsman of Strasburg (he must have had a simple soul, God rest his bones !) had painted a picture of a red chanticleer.

Suzanne coveted this creature. She did not want it to eat. It was evident, therefore, that she desired it because she deemed it beautiful. Her mother, to whom I imparted this simple deduction, answered :

"Stuff and nonsense! If Suzanne had been able to get the plate in her hands, the first thing she would have done would have been to try to put it in her mouth! Upon my word, you clever people have no common sense."

"No doubt she would," I replied; "but what does that prove save that the principal channel of her varied and already numerous faculties is her mouth. She used her mouth before she used her eyes, and quite right, too. At present, her mouth, being cultivated, delicate, and sensitive, is the best organ of perception she has at her disposal. She is quite right to use it. I tell you that your daughter is wisdom personified. She would have put the plate to her mouth, of course she would; but she would have done so because it was beautiful and not because it was good to eat. Observe that this habit, which exists in fact in the case of little children, is still discernible in a figurative sense in the language of grown-up people. We sometimes talk of savouring a poem, a picture, or an opera."

While I was advancing these untenable propositions, which, however, the philosophic world would readily accept provided they were stated in sufficiently unintelligible language, Suzanne was pounding her fists on the plate, scratching it with her nails, speaking to it (and in what pretty,

mysterious babble !), and turning it over every now
and again on its face with a terrific bang.

She did not exhibit any great skill, her move-
ments lacked precision. But, however simple an
action may appear, it is very difficult to perform
until one has acquired the habit of doing it. And
what habits do you expect a fifteen-week-old baby
to have acquired ? Think what a complex apparatus
of nerves, bones, and muscles has to be brought
into play merely to raise your little finger. Pulling
all the strings of Mr. Thomas Holden's marionettes is child's-play to it. Darwin, who was a
sagacious observer, considered it remarkable that
little children should know how to laugh and cry.
He wrote a big book to show how they go about it.
" Nous sommes sans pitié "—we are a hard-hearted
race—" we learned men," as Monsieur Zola says.

Fortunately, I am not quite so profound a savant
as Monsieur Zola. My learning is all on the
surface. I don't go in for experimenting on
Suzanne ; I confine myself to observing what she
does, whenever I can do so without putting her out.

Well, then, she kept scratching away at the
picture on the plate, growing more and more mysti-
fied, for she could not understand how it was that,
if she could see a thing, she could not also take
it in her hands. That was beyond her comprehension, as, indeed, everything else was ; and that

is just what lends Suzanne her charm. Little children pass their days with miracles perpetually taking place around them. To them everything is wonderful, hence the poetry in their eyes. Though they are with us, they dwell in other worlds than ours. The Unknown, the Divine Unknown, is all about them.

"Little stupid!" said her mamma.

"Dear heart, your daughter may be ignorant, but she is perfectly rational. When one sees a thing of beauty, one longs to possess it. That is human nature, and the Law has provided for it. Béranger's gipsies, whose motto is, 'Beholding is holding,' are sages of a very rare order. If every-one thought as they did, there would be no such thing as civilisation, and we should live innocent of clothes and the arts, like the Patagonians. You do not share their views. You have a craving for old tapestry with storks depicted beneath the branches of trees, and you cover every wall in the house with it. I do not quarrel with you, far from it; but do not misconstrue Suzanne and the bird on the plate."

"I understand her well enough. She is just like little Pierre, who wanted the moon in a bucket of water. He didn't get it. But don't tell me, dear, that she takes a painted cock-a-doodle-doo for a real one, for she has never seen one at all."

" No ; she takes an illusion for a reality. And for that, the artists are not a little responsible. It is a long time now since they began to try to portray the world in line and colour. How many thousands of years is it since the death of that worthy cave-dweller who engraved a mammoth—from Nature—on an ivory tusk ? It would be a marvel, and no mistake, if, after all their prolonged efforts in the imitative arts, they could not succeed in deceiving a fifteen-week-old baby. Appearances ! Who is not taken in by them ? Science itself, that is always being thrown at us—does Science go beyond that which *seems* to be ? What does Professor Robin see when he looks into his microscope ? Appearances, nothing but appearances. What says Euripides ? ' We are disquieted in vain by cheating dreams.' "

I was speaking thus, and preparing to comment on this line of Euripides, in which I should no doubt have discovered subtleties that the herb-seller's son had never dreamt of, when the situation suddenly became quite unfavourable to philosophic speculation. For Suzanne, being unsuccessful in her attempts to remove the cock-a-doodle-doo from the plate, threw herself into such a temper, that her face grew as red as a peony, her nostrils dilated like a Kaffir's, her cheeks extended upwards till they nearly blotted out her eyes, and her eyebrows

N

till they climbed to the top of her forehead that had suddenly grown red and was covered all over with bumps and cavities and furrows, till it looked like a tract of volcanic ground. Her mouth opened from ear to ear, and from between the gums there issued the most barbarous of yells.

"There!" I cried; "there we have a manifestation of the passions. But let us not speak ill of the passions; they are the mainspring of all the great deeds that are wrought in this world. In this instance, you observe, they are making a tiny baby almost as redoubtably ugly as a little Chinese idol. Ah! my daughter, you please me well. Let your passions be strong, let them wax greater, and yourself grow stronger with them. And if in after years you become their inexorable mistress, their strength will be your strength, and their loftiness your beauty. The passions make up the whole of man's moral riches."

"Oh! dear! What a din!" exclaimed Suzanne's mother. "What with a philosopher talking nonsense, and a baby that takes a picture on a plate for goodness knows what living thing, one cannot hear one's own voice. We poor women need all our common sense to put up with our husbands and children."

"Your daughter," I replied, "has just made her first essay in the pursuit of the beautiful. A

Romanticist would call it the fascination of the abyss. But I say it is the natural exercise of noble minds. Nevertheless, we must not begin the quest too soon or with too inadequate an equipment. You, dear heart, have a sovereign remedy for Suzanne's troubles. Come! put your child to sleep!"

II

THE STAR

SUZANNE has completed her twelfth month to-night, and during the year that she has been on this old Earth of ours she has passed through a multitude of experiences. A man who could make as many valuable discoveries in twelve years as Suzanne has made in as many months, would be a god among his fellows. Children are neglected geniuses; they seize on the world with superhuman energy. There is nothing comparable to this primal putting forth of vital force, this first upspringing of the soul. Do you realise what it is when these little creatures exercise the faculties of sight and touch, of observation, comparison, and memory? Have you any conception of what walking, coming and going means to them? And, then, their play! Why, there you have the beginning of all the arts. A song and a puppet, a doll and a rhyme, why 'tis nearly the whole of Shakespeare!

Suzanne is the possessor of a great basketful of

toys. Of these, only some, such as the wooden
animals and india-rubber dolls, are toys by nature
and intention. The others merely owe their toy-
like state to a peculiar freak of fortune. These
latter consist of old purses, scraps of lace, the
bottoms of boxes, a yard-measure, a scissor-case,
a tin kettle, a railway guide, and a pebble. They
are one and all pitiably the worse for wear. Every
day Suzanne pulls them out of the basket, one after
another, to give to her mother. She bestows no
exceptional attention on any one of them in particular, and as a rule makes no distinction between
her little stock of possessions and things in general.
For her, the whole world is a great big toy, all
carved and painted.

If you took the trouble to enter into this conception of Nature, and, in the light of it, to inter-
pret all that Suzanne does and thinks, you would
be filled with admiration at the little soul's logic.
But, then, we judge her according to our ideas,
not hers. And because she does not reason like us,
we conclude that she does not reason at all. What
an injustice! I can look at the matter from the
right standpoint, and I can detect the workings of an
ordered intelligence where the vulgar would perceive
nothing but a succession of disconnected actions.

Nevertheless, I dwell in no fool's paradise. I
am not a man who idolises his children. I recog-

nise that my daughter is not so vastly superior to any other child. I do not employ the language of exaggeration in speaking of her. I merely say to her mother :

"My dear, 'tis a very pretty little maid, this little maid of ours."

Her answer somewhat resembles the reply made by Mrs. Primrose when her neighbours paid her a like compliment.

"My friend, Suzanne is what heaven has made her; handsome enough, if she be good enough."

And as she says these words, she looks down long and lovingly at Suzanne, and beneath her drooping lashes one knows her eyes are beaming with pride and adoration.

But I insist.

"Agree that she is pretty," I say.

But she has several reasons for not agreeing, and I know them better than she does herself. She likes to be continually hearing that her child is pretty. Yet, if she said so herself, she would regard it as a little unbecoming, she would deem herself slightly lacking in taste. But, above all, she would fear lest she should offend some mysterious, invisible power, a power which she does not know, but which she feels is at hand, somewhere in the background there, ready to visit on the children the pride of overweening mothers.

And where is the happy man who would not feel a sinking of the heart at the thought of that spectre so surely hiding behind the curtains? And who, at night, as he pressed his wife and child to his breast, would have the courage to say in the presence of the viewless horror, " Dear hearts, how much of our allotted portion of beauty and delight is still in store for us?" Therefore it is that I make reply:

"You are in the right, dear heart, you are ever in the right. Joy has lighted here, beneath this modest roof. Hush, speak softly therefore, lest she spread her wings and fly away. The Athenian mothers used to be afraid of Nemesis, a goddess ever present, never seen. Of her they knew nought save that she was Envy, the envy of the gods; Nemesis, whose handiwork was always to be seen in that mysterious yet familiar thing—ill-luck. Ah! those Athenian mothers. I can see one of them—it is a picture I love to conjure up—I can see her now, stooping down beneath the shade of the laurel where the shrill cicadas sing. I can see her as she lays at the foot of the family altar her little nursling, naked as a baby god. I imagine she was called Lysilla, and that she dreaded Nemesis even as you dread it, my dearest; and that, like you, she was so far from wishing to humiliate other women by a great display of Eastern luxury, that all she thought

of was obtaining pardon for being so happy and so
beautiful. . . . Ah! Lysilla! Lysilla! Have you
then passed away and left behind no shadow of
your shapely form, nor a breath of your gracious
soul? Are you, then, as if you had never been?"

But here Suzanne's mamma slit the thread of
these wayward musings.

"Tell me," she said; "tell me why you speak
thus of this woman. She had her day as we are
having ours. Such is life!"

"Do you imagine, then, my love, that what once
has been can be no more?"

"Precisely. I am not like you, who see marvels
in everything."

All this she said composedly, as she busied herself
making ready to put Suzanne to bed. But Suzanne
obstinately refused to be undressed.

In the annals of old Rome such obstinacy would
be accounted a virtue, a fine trait in the life of a
Titus, say, or a Vespasian, or an Alexander Severus;
but in Suzanne's case it brought her a scolding.
Human Justice, what a mockery thou art! But,
truth to tell, if Suzanne wishes to stay up, it is not
to watch over the safety of the Empire, but to
rummage in the drawer of an old Dutch chest, a
great roomy affair with huge brass handles.

Into it she dives. With one hand she holds on
to the side of the thing to steady herself, and with

the other she seizes bonnets, bodices, dresses, and, uttering all manner of little purling cries the while, casts them with a mighty effort at her feet.

As she stands there, a little lace shawl covering her back, how pathetically comical she looks, and when, every now and then, she turns her head to look at me, the satisfaction that is written on her features is more touching still.

I can restrain myself no longer. " Just look at her ! " I cry, forgetting all about Nemesis ; " how adorable she looks standing at the drawer there."

With a gesture at once mutinous and fearful, her *maman* came and placed a finger on my lips. Then she went back to the ransacked drawer. Meanwhile I resumed my train of thought.

" Dearest, if Suzanne is adorable for what she knows, she is no less so for what she does not know. It is when her knowledge fails that her poetry is revealed."

At this Suzanne's mamma turned her eyes upon me, smiling a little mocking smile out of the corner of her mouth.

" Suzanne's poetry," she cried ; " your daughter's poetry? Why, she's only happy when she's in the kitchen, that daughter of yours. I found her grubbing among the potato peelings the other day as happy as a queen. You call that poetry, do you ? "

"Most certainly, my dear, most certainly! All
Nature is mirrored in her eyes with so magnificent
a purity that for her nothing in the world is dirty,
not even the refuse-basket. Therefore it is that
you discovered her rapt in wondering admiration
of cabbage leaves, onion skin, and shrimps' tails.
It was a delicious experience for her. I assure you
she transmutes Nature with heavenly alchemy, and
whatsoever she sees or touches is instinct with
beauty in her eyes."

During this harangue Suzanne quitted her chest
of drawers and went to the window. Her mother
followed her and took her in her arms. The
lovely tresses of the acacia whose blossom lay in
trails of white about our courtyard were bathed
in the translucent darkness. The dog was sleeping
with his front paws outside his kennel. Far off the
earth lay drenched in liquid azure. We all three
held our peace.

Then, amid the silence, the majestic silence of
the night, Suzanne raised her arm as high as she
could above her, and with her finger, which she could
never stretch quite straight, she pointed to a star.
This finger—a miracle of tiny loveliness—she would
bend at intervals as though she were beckoning to
something.

Then Suzanne talked to the star.

What she told it was not made up of words;

it was a language obscure and lovely, a sort of strange runic chant, something sweet yet profoundly mysterious, as is befitting to express the soul of a baby, when a star is mirrored in it.

"What a queer little thing it is!" said her mother, giving her a hug.

III

GUIGNOL

YESTERDAY I took Suzanne to see Guignol. We both derived much pleasure from our visit. It is a performance within our intellectual compass. Were I a dramatic author I should write for marionettes. I don't know whether I should have sufficient talent to succeed ; but, at all events, the task would not oppress me with alarm. But to compose sentences for the cultured lips of the fair comediennes of the Comédie Française ! I should never be daring enough for that. And then the drama—the grown-up people's idea of it, I mean—is too infinitely complicated a thing for me. I can simply make nothing of those highly involved intrigues that are all the craze just now. My whole art would consist in depicting the passions, and those of the simplest. That kind of thing would not do for the Gymnase, the Vaudeville, or the Français ; but it would be first-rate for Guignol.

That is the place for strong and simple passions.

The truncheon is their most ordinary instrument, and it cannot be doubted that the truncheon possesses conspicuous advantages from the comic point of view : an admirable agent is the truncheon, and gives no end of go to the play as it hurries on to the grand rough-and-tumble at the finish —the "grand charassement final," as the Lyons folk, with whom these performances originated, call the general mêlée with which they invariably conclude. A fatal, an everlasting affair, this "grand charassement." 'Tis the 10th August! 'Tis the 9th Thermidor! 'Tis Waterloo!

Well, I was telling you, I took Suzanne to Guignol yesterday. No doubt the piece had its shortcomings. I found it remarkably rich in obscurities ; but it was splendidly calculated to commend itself to the contemplative mind : it provided such plentiful food for thought. According to my view of it, the play is of the philosophic order. The characters are true to life, and they act with vigour. I will tell you the plot just as I heard it.

When the curtain went up, we saw Guignol himself appear on the scene. I recognised him : it was certainly he. His broad, placid face still showed the marks of the thwacks that had flattened his nose, though without marring the friendly ingenuousness of his look and smile.

He was not wearing the serge gaberdine or the cotton bonnet which in 1815 no citizen of Lyons could behold on the *Allée des Botteaux* without laughing. But if some survivor of those little boys who, away back in 1815, had seen both Guignol and Napoleon on the banks of the Rhone, had come, before dying of old age, and sat down beside us yesterday in the *Champs Elysées*, he would have recognised the famous "salsify" of his beloved marionette, the little pigtail which danced and jigged so comically at the back of Guignol's neck. The rest of the costume—green coat and black cocked hat—was in keeping with the old Parisian tradition which represents Guignol as a kind of valet.

Guignol looked at us with his great eyes, and I was at once taken with his air of impudent candour and that transparent simplicity of soul which imparts innocence to vice itself. As far as soul and expression went, it was the same old Guignol that the worthy Mourguet of Lyons played with such infinite jest and excellent fancy. I could almost hear him saying to his proprietor, Monsieur Canezou, who had declared his stories were enough to send a man to sleep standing up:

"You're right, let's go home to bed."

So far, our Guignol had said nothing. But his little pigtail was a-dance at the back of his neck, and everyone had begun to laugh.

Then Gringalet, his son, arrived on the scene, and rammed his head with fascinating grace into the paternal abdomen. The audience were not indignant; on the contrary, they roared with laughter.

Such a début is the last word in dramatic art. And in case you don't know how it came about that this piece of audacity was such a success, I will tell you. Guignol is a valet, and wears a livery. Gringalet, his son, wears a blouse. He is no man's servant, and he does no work. This superiority enables him to misuse his father without offending the public's sense of propriety.

Mademoiselle Suzanne recognised this immediately, and her affection for Gringalet suffered no abatement. Indeed, Gringalet is the sort of person you can't help liking. He is thin and weedy, but he is full of resource. Gringalet is the man who jumps on the policeman. Mademoiselle Suzanne, who is six years old, has quite made up her mind regarding the representatives of law and order. She is "agin" them, and shakes her sides when Pandore gets a drubbing. Oh! it is very wrong of her, no doubt. Still, I confess I should be sorry to have it otherwise. I like people to have something of the rebel in them, no matter what age they be. I myself am a peaceable citizen, a great respecter of authority, a most humble observer of the law. Nevertheless, if I saw someone play off a good trick on a gendarme or a sub-prefect or a park-keeper, I should be the first to laugh at it. But, let me see, we were talking about the tussle between Guignol and Gringalet.

Mademoiselle Suzanne takes Gringalet's part, and I Guignol's. You shall hear both sides and judge for yourself. Guignol and Gringalet have long been making for a mysterious village, known only to themselves—the sort of village that would attract a wild rush of greedy desperadoes if they only knew of its existence. But this village was more difficult to find than the palace of the Sleeping Beauty that lay undiscovered for a hundred years. There was a certain spice of magic in the matter, for the region was inhabited by an Enchanter, an Enchanter who had a treasure which he had promised to bestow on whomsoever should emerge triumphant from divers trials, the very thought of which made your blood curdle. Our two travellers made their way into the enchanted region with very dissimilar ideas. Guignol is weary; he lies down to sleep. His son upbraids him for his lack of grit.

"Is this how we are going to gain possession of the treasure which we have set out to seek?"

And Guignol answers:

"Is there a treasure to compare with sleep?"

I like that reply. I behold in Guignol a sage who has realised the vanity of all things, and whose

sole desire is to enjoy repose after the sinful or
bootless tumults of the world. But Mademoiselle
Suzanne looks upon him as a muddy-mettled rascal
who goes to sleep when he ought to be up and
doing, who will perhaps be the cause of their losing
the things which they had set out to find—lovely
things, too, perhaps—ribbons, cakes, and flowers!
She applauds the zealous Gringalet, untiring in
his quest of these glorious treasures.

As I have said, the trials they have to undergo
are terrible. They have to face a crocodile and slay
the Devil.

"There's the Devil!" said I to Suzanne.

"That! why, that's a black man!" she replied.

This was rationalism pure and simple, and I was
in despair. But I knew better, and I remained an
interested spectator of the battle between Gringalet
and the Devil. It is an awful struggle, and it ends
with the death of the Devil. Gringalet kills him.

Frankly, I don't look on that as his most laudable
achievement. I can quite understand how some of
the audience, possessed of superior spiritual insight
to Mam'zelle Suzanne's, looked on it coldly, nay,
with some degree of disapproval. For, look you,
the Devil being dead, it would be good-bye to sin.
Perhaps Beauty, the Devil's ally, would go with him.
Perhaps we should never more behold the flowers
that enchant us, and the eyes for love of which we

would lay down our lives. What, if that be so,
what in the world would become of us? Should
we still be able to practise virtue? I doubt it.
Gringalet did not sufficiently realise that evil is as
necessary a corollary of good as darkness is of light,
that virtue is wholly in the effort, and that if there
were no longer any Devil to fight against, the saints
would be just as much out of work as the sinners.
Everyone would be bored to death. I am sure that,
when he killed the Devil, Gringalet committed an
act of grave imprudence.

Well, Punchinello came on and made his bow,
the curtain fell, and all the little boys and girls
went home; but still I sat on, deep in meditation.
Mam'zelle Suzanne, perceiving my thoughtful mien,
concluded that I was in trouble. It is a common
notion that it is only unhappy people who think.

Very delicately and tenderly she put her hand in
mine, and asked me what I was grieving for.

I confessed that I was worried at Gringalet's
having killed the Devil.

Thereupon she twined her little arms about my
neck, and, putting her lips to my ear, she whispered:
"Let me tell you something; Gringalet killed the
black man, but not for good."

My misgivings vanished: "The Devil is not
dead!" said I to myself; and we departed happy
in our minds.

SUZANNE'S FRIENDS

I

ANDRÉ

YOU knew Doctor Trévière? You remember his frank, open countenance, and his fine blue eyes? He had the skill and the soul of a great surgeon. People used to speak with admiration of his presence of mind in critical circumstances. One day, when he was performing a big operation in the theatre, the patient fell into a state of collapse. His temperature dropped suddenly, his pulse became imperceptible. The man's life was ebbing away. But Trévière picked him up in both arms, gripped him to his breast, and shook his gashed and bleeding body as a wrestler might shake his antagonist. Then he laid him back on the operating table, and, resuming his scalpel, proceeded to handle it with his customary boldness and precision. The man's circulation was restored and his life was saved.

As soon as the apron was put aside, Trévière was once more the good-hearted, simple-minded individual he ordinarily was. People liked to hear his great, honest laugh. A few months after the operation I have just mentioned, Trévière pricked his finger wiping his bistoury. He didn't think it worth worrying about, but he contracted blood poisoning, and in two days he was dead. He was only thirty-six, and he left a wife and child to whom he had been passionately devoted.

Every day when the weather was warm and sunny a young woman in deep mourning might have been seen seated beneath the fir-trees in the Bois de Boulogne knitting and looking over her needles at a little boy crawling about on all fours amid wheelbarrow, spade, and little mounds of earth. It was Madame Trévière. The sunlight fell caressingly on the warm pallor of her features. Now and then a deep sigh would escape her, or a glance steal from her great brown eyes in whose depths there floated tiny motes of gold—a sigh and a glance that told of the full, pent-up life within. Her eyes lingered lovingly on her little boy, who, from time to time, to draw attention to the mud pies he had made, would lift up his head of auburn hair and display a pair of blue eyes, the hair and eyes of his father.

His face was pink and chubby. But he began to lose flesh as he grew taller, and the colour faded from his cheeks. His mother began to feel anxious about him. Sometimes, while he was running about the wood with his little playmates, he would brush by the chair where she was knitting; then seizing hold of him as he flew past, she would lift up his chin, and knit her brows as she anxiously scanned his little pale face. Then she would release him and gaze after him with an almost imperceptible shake of the head as he resumed his flight. At night she would get up if she heard the smallest noise and stand barefooted leaning over his little bed. Some of her husband's old medical friends told her there was nothing to be alarmed at: the child was delicate, that was all, and he must have pure country air.

So Madame Trévière packed up her things and went down to Bolles to her husband's people, who were small farmers there. Trévière, you know, was a countryman's son, and, till he was twelve, he had been a rare hand at bird's-nesting coming home from school.

The greetings took place beneath the hams that hung from the smoke-begrimed roof of the living-room. Granny Trévière was stooping down in front of the great open hearth, and, still retaining her hold on the handle of the frying-pan, turned a mistrustful eye on the Parisienne and her maid, But she pronounced the boy "a dear little fellow. and the very image of his father"—while goodman Trévière, a little awkward and unbending, in clothes of coarse homespun, was "very pleased to see his grandson André."

But before supper was over, André was giving his grandpapa great big kisses, and grandpapa's beard was "oh, so dreadfully prickly." Then he stood straight up on the old fellow's knees, and, digging his fist into his cheeks, wanted to know why they were so hollow.

"Because I've got no teeth," was the reply.

"And why haven't you any teeth?"

"Because they turned black, and I sowed them in the furrow to see if I could manage to grow some white ones."

Whereat André laughed consumedly. His grandfather's cheeks were very different from his mother's.

It had been arranged that the Parisian dame and her little boy were to have the best bedroom—the room with the bridal bed, which the worthy couple had only slept in once, and the oak chest stuffed full of linen, which was always kept locked. The little cot, which had once been their own son's, had been brought down from the attic for their grandson. It had been put up in the most sheltered corner of the room, under a shelf laden with pots of jam. Like a methodical woman, Madame Trévière made innumerable little voyages of discovery over the creaking deal floor, but she was fated to find never a hook to hang a dress on.

The walls and the ceiling, with its great wooden beams, were all whitewashed. Madame Trévière paid scant attention to the coloured prints that adorned the walls of this grand room, but over the bridal bed her eyes lighted upon a picture of some little children in black jackets with badges on the arm, and white knickerbockers, bearing tapers, and filing into a Gothic church. Underneath was engraved the following legend, the names, date, and signature being filled in by hand: " I, the undersigned, hereby certify that Pierre Agénor Trévière made his first Communion in the Parish Church at Bolles on the 15th May 1849. Gontard, Curé."

As she read these words, the widow heaved a sigh, the sigh of a brave, sensible woman, one of those sighs which, with the tears of love, are the most priceless of earthly treasures.

Then she undressed André.

" Come, say your prayers," said she.

" Mamma, I do love you so," he murmured; after which act of devotion he drooped his head, closed his little fists, and fell peacefully asleep.

Next morning, when he woke, he discovered the existence of the farm-yard. He was filled with wonder and delight. He looked out on the fowls, the cow, the old one-eyed horse, and the pig. The pig was a special attraction. The fascination lasted for days and days, and it was the most difficult thing in the world to get him to come in to meals, and when he did appear, he was covered with straw and manure, his hair was all cobwebs, his boots soaking with dirty stable water, his knees barked, but his cheeks as red as roses, and he himself as happy as a sandboy.

"Keep away from me, you little horror!" his mother cried, and forthwith smothered him with kisses.

As he sat at table perched on the edge of a form, eating away at the leg of a chicken, he looked like a diminutive Hercules devouring his club.

He seemed to eat without noticing it, forgot to drink anything, and prattled unceasingly.

"Mamma, what's a green chicken called?" said André.

"Why, you must have seen a parrakeet," his mother returned thoughtlessly.

That's how it came about that André dubbed his grandfather's ducks parrakeets, a circumstance that rendered his vivid narratives a trifle puzzling.

But it was no easy task to get a rise out of André.

"Mamma!" he exclaimed; "do you know what grandpapa told me? He said that it was the fowls who made the eggs. But I know it isn't. I know quite well that the greengrocer in the *Avenue de Neuilly* makes the eggs and then takes them to the fowls to be warmed. Because, mamma, how could fowls make eggs, when they haven't got any hands to make them with?"

And so André prosecuted his researches into the mysteries of Nature. When he went for walks in the woods with his mother, he experienced all the sensations of Robinson Crusoe. One day, while Madame Trévière was sitting beneath an oak-tree by the roadside working at her knitting, he found a mole, a very big mole. True, it was a dead mole; it even had some blood on its muzzle. "André," exclaimed his mother, "will you leave those horrible things alone? . . . Oh! quick! look there, in the tree!"

He looked, and saw a squirrel hopping about among the branches. His mamma was right: a live squirrel is worth a dead mole, any day.

But it was gone too soon, and André was asking whether squirrels have wings, when a passer-by, whose frank, manly face was fringed with a fine brown beard, raised his straw hat and approached Madame Trévière.

"Good morning, madame! How do you do? Fancy our meeting again! That is your little boy? A nice little fellow. They told me you were down here staying with Gaffer Trévière . . . I beg your pardon, but, you see, I've known him so many years."

"We came because my little boy was in need of fresh air. But I remember you here long ago, when my husband was alive." There was a quiver in the young widow's voice as she uttered these words ; and he said, gravely :

"I understand, madame," and, quite simply, he bowed his head as though to salute the memory of a great sorrow.

Then, after a pause, he continued :

"Those were great times. What a number of good folk have died since then. My poor artists, my poor Millet. Ah! well! I am still the 'painters' friend,' as they call me down at Barbizon. I knew them all, and capital fellows they were, too."

"And your factory?"

"My factory! Oh! that is going on swimmingly."

"Oh! mamma, mamma!" cried André, rushing in betwixt them. "There are ever so many ladybirds under a big stone. There's at least a million of them, really!"

"Be quiet! Run away and play!" said his mother, curtly.

The painters' friend took up the conversation again in his full rich voice.

"How pleasant it is to meet again. My friends often ask me what has become of the beautiful Madame Trévière. I shall tell them that the beautiful Madame Trévière is still beautiful—more beautiful than ever, in fact. Au revoir! madame."

"Good-bye! Monsieur Lassalle."

Then André came on the scene again.

"Mamma," said he, "why do they only call lady-birds the good God's beasties. Are not all insects the good God's beasties? Are there Devil's beasties too, mamma? Why don't you tell me?" and he tugged at her skirt.

Then she scolded him.

"André, you must not interrupt when I am talking to people, do you hear?"

"Why not?"

"Because it is rude."

Then there were a few tears, that ended in smiles and kisses. This was another happy day, one of the days that remind you of the skies that hang low over hill and dale—moist skies shot through with rays of sunlight, skies that bring sadness and charm to the heart.

Not long afterwards, one very wet day, Monsieur Lassalle came to call on the young widow.

"Good-morning, madame! Ah! Père Trévière, why, you look heartier than ever!"

"The carcase is still right enough," said the old man; "but the legs are done for."

"And you, mother? Always got your nose

over the saucepan, eh? Testing the soup? All the good cooks do that."

These familiarities made the old woman smile, and the eyes in her wrinkled old face gleamed with a merry twinkle.

He took André on his knee, and pinched his cheeks; but the child quickly tore himself away, and rushed over to clamber up on his grandfather's knee.

"You be the horse!" he cried. "I'm the postillion. Gee up, there! Get along with you!"

The visit went off without the widow and the visitor exchanging half a dozen words, but many a time glances passed between them like the lightning that flashes betwixt earth and sky on warm summer nights.

"Do you know much about that gentleman, papa?" asked the young woman, with an assumed air of unconcern.

"Know him! I knew him before he was breeched; and his father before him! Why, everyone knew him for miles around. And fine people they are, all fair and square and above-board. They're well off, too: Monsieur Philippe (that's what we call him) doesn't employ less than threescore workmen in that factory of his."

André now deemed the moment ripe for him to express his view.

" He's a horrid man ! " said he.

His mother told him sharply that if he was only going to talk nonsense, he had better hold his tongue altogether.

Thenceforth fate willed that Madame Trévière should encounter Monsieur Lassalle at every turn in the road.

She became restless, absent, dreamy. She trembled at the sound of the wind among the leaves. Her knitting was left half finished, and she acquired a habit of sitting with her chin resting in the hollow of her hand.

One evening, in the autumn, a great gale arose blowing in from the sea. It swept wailing and howling over Père Trévière's house, and over all the surrounding country. The young widow hastily dismissed the servant who had been lighting the fire, and began to put André to bed. While she was pulling off his woollen stockings and patting his little cold feet with the palm of her hand, he, hearing the hollow roar of the wind and the rattle of the rain against the window, flung his arms round his mother's neck as she was bending over him.

" Mother," said he, " I am frightened."

" There, there, never mind," said she, soothingly, giving him a kiss.

And she went and sat down by the fire and began to read a letter.

As she read on, the colour came into her cheeks; her bosom heaved with warm sighs. And when she had finished reading, she remained lying back in her arm-chair with listless hands, lost in a dream.

"He loves me ; he is so kind, so frank, so good. It is dreary to be alone these winter evenings. He treated me so delicately ; certainly he has a kind heart. The way he proposed to me gives me sufficient proof of that."

Her glance fell on the "first communion" picture: "I, the undersigned, certify that Pierre Agénor Trévière . . ."

She lowered her eyes. Then she let her thoughts run on again :

"A woman can't bring up a boy all by herself—André shall have a father . . ."

"Mamma !"

The cry came from the little bed, and made her start and tremble.

"What do you want me for, André? You are very restless to-night."

"Mamma, I was thinking about something."

"Instead of going to sleep—and what were you thinking about ? "

"Papa is dead, isn't he ? "

"Yes, my poor child."

"Then he will never come back again ? "

"No, my darling."

"Well, mamma, it's a good thing, after all. Because, you see, I love you so much. I love you like two people, and if he came back I shouldn't have any love left for him at all."

She looked at him long and anxiously, then threw herself back again in the arm-chair, where she remained motionless with her head in her hands.

The child had been asleep more than two hours, lulled by the sound of the wind, when she drew near him and murmured with a deep sigh:

"Sleep on ; he will not come back."

Nevertheless, when two months were over, he did come back, and he came back with the broad, sunburnt features of Monsieur Lassalle, the new master of the house. And little André began to grow sallow and thin and listless.

He is cured again now. He loves his nurse with the love he used to bestow on his mother ; but he doesn't know that his nurse has got a young man.

II

PIERRE

HOW old is your little boy, madame?"
The mother looked at her child as
one would look at a clock to see the
time, and replied :

"Pierre! He is just twenty-nine
months, madame."

It would have done just as well to say two and
a half; but Pierre is very sharp, and does a world
of remarkable things for his age, and there would be
a risk of other mothers being a shade less jealous if
he were represented as slightly older, and therefore
slightly less of a prodigy, than he actually is. She
has yet another reason for not wishing to make
Pierre a day older than his real age : she wishes
him to remain her little one, her little baby boy.
She feels that, little by little, he is slipping away
from her. Ungrateful little beings, they are always
bent on cutting themselves adrift. The primal
separation dates from their birth, for what, alas!
has a mother then but her breast and her two
arms to hold her baby to her.

Therefore, Pierre is just precisely twenty-nine months old. But it is a fine age that! I look on it with very considerable respect. I have several friends of that age who behave most handsomely towards me. Still, none of them are gifted with Pierre's imagination. Pierre displays extraordinary facility and some capriciousness in garnering his ideas. Some of them date from a remote past. He remembers faces that he has not seen for a month or more, and he discerns in the picture-books people give him a thousand and one peculiarities that charm and excite him. When he is turning over the one he likes best—the one with only half its pages torn—two red spots appear on his cheeks, and his eyes grow morbidly bright.

His mother is afraid of that hectic colour and those bright eyes. She is terrified lest his little brain should be overwrought; she thinks of fever and all kinds of things. Sometimes she almost wishes he were like the baker's little boy, whom she sees every day sitting outside the shop, with a great flat face, expressionless blue eyes, a mouth lost to view beneath a pair of fat cheeks, and a general air of stupidity and health. There was no need for that boy's mother to be anxious about him, at any rate. But Pierre! his colour keeps coming and going, his little hands are burning hot, and he keeps turning and twisting about in his cot the whole night long.

The doctor, too, does not approve of our little one looking at pictures. He says he should have nothing to excite him. "Bring him up like a puppy," says he; "there's nothing very difficult about that."

Therein he errs, for it is a very difficult thing indeed. The doctor knows nothing about the psychology of a little boy of twenty-nine months. And is the doctor so sure that puppies do grow up without mental excitement? I knew one—he was about six weeks old—who used to dream the whole night through, and fell from laughter to tears with the most distressing rapidity. He used to fill my room with noises that indicated a highly disordered imagination. There wasn't much calmness about him. No, indeed!

And the little animal began to grow thin, like Pierre. Nevertheless he went on living. In the same way, Pierre has plenty of generous vitality in him; there is nothing organically wrong. But it would be good to see him less thin and pale.

Paris doesn't suit this little Parisian. Not that he doesn't like it there. On the contrary, the trouble is that he has too much to amuse him, too much variety of colour and movement, too many appeals to his imagination and his understanding; he wears himself out with it all.

Last July his mother took him—a poor, pinched,

pale-faced little fellow—to some quiet spot in Switzerland, where he could see nothing but the pines upon the mountain side, the green pastures, and cows browsing in the valley below.

For three months he rested on the bosom of the great tranquil Nurse, three smiling months of happiness, and unlimited brown bread. When he came back in the early part of October, it was a new Pierre that I beheld : a little gold and brown, almost chubby-faced, Pierre, with swarthy hands, a fine, sturdy voice, and a hearty laugh.

"Look at Pierre! Look what a fright he is!" said the happy mother. "He has a face like a Dutch doll."

But the colour did not last. He grew pale, fragile, and excitable again, with something too suggestive of the rare exotic about him. Once more Paris began to exert its influence ; and when I say Paris, I mean the spiritual, not the material Paris—the Paris that is everywhere and nowhere, Paris that fills one with a vague yearning, that makes one restless and eager, and sets the brain at work, even when one is quite a little child.

And so here was Pierre flushing and turning pale over his picture-books in the old way again. About the end of that December I found him nervous as ever, with great dilated eyes and burning hands. He slept poorly and didn't relish his food.

"It is nothing," said the doctor; "give him plenty to eat."

Yes, but how? His poor mother had worried herself about him till she wept, but to no purpose.

Christmas Eve brought Pierre dolls and horses and soldiers galore. In the morning his mother was standing despondently in her dressing-gown in front of the fireplace looking doubtfully at this varied assortment of playthings.

"All these things will excite him more than ever," she said to herself; "there are too many of them." And softly, so as not to disturb Pierre, she took Punch—who had a wicked leer in his eyes—the soldiers, which she feared might lure her boy to the battle-field one day, she even took the good red horse, and, piling them up in her arms, went on tip-toe and hid them in her cupboard.

She left but one thing in the fireplace, and that was a white deal box, an eighteenpenny sheep-run that some poor man had sent him. Then she went and sat down by the little bed and gazed at her boy. Being a woman, the little deception involved in her beneficent action rather took her fancy, and she smiled. Then her glance lighted on the blue lines round her baby's eyes, and she said to herself, "What a dreadful thing it is, that we cannot get the child to eat."

No sooner was he dressed than little Pierre opened the box and saw the sheep, the cows, the horses, and the trees, little curly trees. To be accurate, it was a farm-yard rather than a sheep-run.

He saw the farmer and the farmer's wife. The farmer was carrying a scythe, his wife a rake. They were going to the meadow to make hay, but they did not look as if they were walking. The farmer's wife had on a straw hat and a red dress. Pierre kissed her several times, and the paint came off on his face. Then he looked at the house. It was so small and so low that the farmer's wife could not possibly have stood upright in it; but it had a door, and that was how Pierre knew it was a house.

How do such things mirror themselves in the primitive unjaded eyes of a little child? Whatever the effect, there was, in this instance, enchantment in it. He grasped them in his little fists, and made his hands all sticky. He set them out on his little table, and called them by name in accents of fond affection: "Dada! Toutou! Moumou!" He picked up one of the remarkable trees with its slim, straight bole and conical crest, and said, "A pine!" It was a sort of revelation for his mother. She would never have guessed it. Why, of course, what could a green tree with a conical crest and a straight stem be, but a pine? Still, she would never have recognised it unless Pierre had told her.

"You angel!" she exclaimed; and gave him such a hug that the sheep-run was three parts upset.

Meanwhile, Pierre went on discovering resemblances between the trees in the box and the trees which he had seen away among the mountains.

He saw other things, too, which his mother did not see. All those little pieces of painted wood brought back sweet visions to his mind. By their means he passed his days with the Alps once more around him; he was back again in Switzerland, where he had been wont to eat so well. One idea led to another, and he began to think about food.

"I should like some bread and milk," said he.

He ate and drank. His appetite came back. Next day he looked at the sheep-run, and felt hungry again. See what it is to have imagination! A fortnight later he had grown into a sturdy little fellow once more. His mother was in raptures.

"Look," she said, "look! what cheeks! And it's all due to poor Mr. Blank's sheep-run!"

III

JESSY

THERE dwelt in London, in the reign of Elizabeth, one Bog, a man of learning, who, under the name of Bogus, had gained much renown by reason of a Treatise concerning Human Error, which no one had read.

Bogus, who had wrought thereat for twenty-five years, had as yet given none of it to the public; but his manuscript, writ fair and ranged on shelves in a window recess, consisted of no less than ten folio volumes. Of these, the first treated of the error of coming into the world—the primary error from which all other errors do proceed. The subsequent volumes dealt with the errors of little boys and girls, of youthful folk, of those of riper years, and of the aged; of the errors committed by persons of divers occupations, such as statesmen, merchants, soldiers, cooks, politicians, and so forth. The concluding volumes—as yet unfinished—were made up of observations concerning the errors of the body politic, which errors do arise from, and

have their origin in, the errors committed by the
individuals, or groups of individuals, composing it.
And so perfect was the interdependence, one upon
another, of the arguments in this great work, that
no single page could be extracted therefrom without destroying the continuity of the whole. The
proofs followed orderly, one after another, and the
final demonstration established beyond all contro-
versy that evil is the essence of life, and that if life
be a quantity it may be affirmed with mathemati-
cal accuracy that the amount of evil upon the
earth is co-extensive with the amount of life
existing upon it.

Bogus had not committed the error of getting
married. He lived alone in his humble abode with
an old housekeeper called Kat, that is Catherine.
He used to call her Clausentina, because she came
from Southampton, a town which is the successor
to the Roman station of Clausentum.

But his sister, whose mind was of a less transcendental cast than her brother's, had perpetrated
a whole series of errors, for she had fallen in
love with a city cloth merchant, espoused the said
merchant, and brought into the world a little
daughter, whose name was Jessy. Her crowning
error had been to die after ten years of married life,
thus causing the death of the cloth merchant, who
found it impossible to live without her. Bogus

took the little orphan girl into his house out of pity, and also because he hoped that she would provide him with some valuable material for that section of his work which treated of the errors of children.

She was then six years of age. For the first eight days she was with the sage she wept and said nothing. On the ninth, she addressed Bog as follows :

"I have seen mamma; she was dressed all in white; she was wearing flowers in a fold of her dress; she scattered them upon my bed, but I could not find them this morning. Give them to me ; give me mamma's flowers!"

Bog recorded this error, but he noted in his commentary thereon that the error was innocent and not wholly unpleasing.

Some time after this, Jessy came to Bog and said : "Uncle Bog, you are old and you are ugly; but I love you, and you must love me."

Whereupon Bog took up his pen, but, recognising, after some conflict of mind, that he no longer presented a very youthful appearance, and that he never had been particularly handsome, he refrained from recording the child's remark. He merely said :

"Why must I love you, Jessy?"

"Because I am little," was the reply.

"Is it so?" Bog wondered; "is it, then, true that we ought to love the little ones? Peradventure it is, for in good sooth they stand in great need of love. This would excuse the error common to mothers, who give to their little ones both their milk and their love. Here, methinks, is one chapter in my Treatise that I shall have to rewrite."

When, on the morning of his birthday, he went into the room where he kept his books and papers, he became aware of a pleasant smell, and he beheld a pot of carnations on his window-ledge.

There were but three flowers, but their hue was scarlet, and the sunlight shone pleasantly upon them. And everything was smiling in this learned chamber; the old tapestry arm-chair, the walnut table, even the ancient books in their dingy bindings of calf and vellum and pigskin looked down with smiles; and even Bogus, withered and dried up as they, began to smile too.

"Look, uncle Bog!" said Jessy, giving him a kiss. "This is Heaven here" (and she pointed through the little leaded panes to the misty blue of the outer air); "then here, lower down, is the Earth, the Earth in blossom" (and she pointed to the pot of pinks); "and then here, down below, where these big black books are, this is Hell."

These "big black books" were nothing more nor less than the ten volumes of the Treatise on

Human Error ranged along in the space under the window. This error of Jessy's reminded the doctor of his work, which he had neglected of late in order to take Jessy for walks in the streets and gardens. In the course of these wanderings, Jessy discovered a thousand delightful things, and she proceeded to make them known to Bogus, who had scarcely put his head out of doors in his life before.

He used to go back to his manuscripts, but somehow he no longer felt at home in his work. Jessy and the flowers alike were lacking.

By good fortune, philosophy came to his rescue at this juncture, and suggested the highly transcendental idea that Jessy served no useful purpose in the world, a truth to which he clung with tenacity because it was essential to the maintenance of his Theory.

It chanced that one day, when his thoughts were running on this theme, he discovered Jessy in his library threading a needle by the window where the carnations were. He asked her what she wanted to sew.

"What! Uncle Bog," said Jessy; "don't you know that the swallows have flown away?"

Bogus knew nothing about it, for the matter was not dealt with in Pliny or in Avicenna.

"Yes," continued Jessy; "Kat told me yesterday."

"Kat!" cried Bogus; "does the child speak thus of the worthy Clausentina?"

"Kat said to me yesterday, 'The swallows have flown away earlier than usual this year; we shall have an early winter, and a hard one.' That is what Kat said, and, then, I saw mother. She was in white, and there was a brightness about her hair. Only she had no flowers this time. She said to me, 'Jessy, you must take Uncle Bog's fur cloak from the press and mend it if it requires it.' I awoke, and as soon as I was dressed, I took the cloak from the press, and, as it is torn in several places, I am going to mend it."

Winter came, and fulfilled the prediction of the swallows. Bogus in his cloak, with his feet by the fire, sat striving to patch up some of the chapters of his Treatise; but every time he managed to reconcile his new experiences with his Theory of the Universality of Evil, Jessy perhaps would bring him a jug of good ale, or merely show her eyes and her smiling face, and all his theories would be blown to the winds once more.

When summer came again, uncle and niece went for rambles in the country. Jessy used to bring back flowers and herbs with her, and of an evening her uncle would sit by her and tell her their names, while she would arrange them according to their properties. One evening, as she was spreading out on the table the flowers which she had gathered during the day, she spoke to Bogus, saying : " Now, Uncle Bog, I know the names of all the plants that you have shown me. Here are those which heal and console. I wish to keep them in order that I may always know them, and that I may make them known to others. But I want a big book to press them in."

" Take this one," said Bog.

And he pointed to the first volume of the Treatise on Human Error.

When this volume had a plant on every page, they went on to the next, and in three summers the Doctor's *magnum opus* had been completely changed into an herbarium.

SUZANNE'S LIBRARY

Q

I

TO MADAME D——

Paris, 15th December 188–.

EW Year's Day is nearly here. It is the day for presents and good wishes, and of them the children have the lion's share. And that is perfectly natural. They have need of our love. And they possess the special charm—of poverty. Even children that are born in luxury have nought but what is given them. Then, again, they do not make us presents in return, and that is why it is so nice to give them things.

There is nothing more interesting than choosing toys and books for children. Some day or other, I shall write a philosophic treatise on children's toys. It is a subject that has great attractions for me ; but I should not dare to attempt it without long and serious preparation.

To-day I shall confine myself to speaking of the books designed to afford amusement to children ; and, since you have been good enough to ask me to do so, I will acquaint you with some of my ideas upon the subject.

There is one question which calls for an answer at the outset. Ought we, in making presents of books to children, to give a preference to books written expressly for them? To enable us to answer this, our own experience is sufficient. It is a remarkable fact that, in the vast majority of cases, children display a marked antipathy to books "for the young." The reason for this is only too evident. They perceive, as soon as they have read a page or two, that the author has endeavoured to enter into their world instead of transporting them into his own; and they realise in consequence that they cannot, under his guidance, expect to find a means of gratifying that passion for the novel and the unknown which animates mankind at every age. Little things though they be, they are already possessed by that hunger for knowledge which makes the student and the poet. They long for someone to lay bare the secrets of the Universe, the hidden, mystic Universe. The writer that throws them back on themselves, and insists on their contemplating their own childishness, bores them beyond endurance. This, however, is what people who write for the young are always endeavouring to do. They aim at putting themselves into the position of little children. They become children, but with none of a child's innocence or grace. I remember a story—something about a fire at school—that someone gave me once, no doubt with the best intentions in the world I was only seven, and yet I felt it was sorry stuff. Another such story would have disgusted me with books altogether, yet I adored reading.

But you will say one must respect the limits of a child's understanding.

That is doubtless true, but only indifferent success is achieved by the method ordinarily followed, a method which consists in putting on a sort of goody-goody, namby-pamby tone, in talking ineffectively about feeble things ; in voluntarily laying aside, in a word, all those things which in the case of grown-up people tend to charm or to persuade.

Nothing appeals to the juvenile mind like a noble genius. The books which little boys and girls love best are lofty works, rich in high conceptions—works whose component parts are so finely and deftly arranged that they shine forth in one luminous whole, books that are written in a style fraught alike with energy and meaning.

I have often given quite young children some passages from the *Odyssey* to read in a good translation. They were delighted. If we leave out some very considerable portions, there is

nothing better for a child of twelve to steep his
soul in than *Don Quixote*. Myself, I have read
the great-hearted Cervantes off and on ever since
I learned to read at all ; and so warmly did I love
him, so thoroughly did I enter into his spirit,
that it is to him I owe a great measure of
that cheery mental outlook which I still possess
to-day.

Robinson Crusoe itself, which, for a hundred
years or more, has been the classic among children's
books, was primarily written for grave men,
merchants of the city of London, and the mariners
of his Majesty's navy. Into this work its author
put all his art, all his intellectual directness, all
his immense knowledge and experience. And in
the end it turned out to be just the thing for a
schoolboy's delectation.

The masterpieces that I have mentioned all have
a story to unfold ; they tell about people, and
what befel them. The finest book in all the
world would convey nothing to a child if its ideas
were expressed in the form of abstractions. The
faculty of thinking in the abstract, and of com-
prehending abstractions, develops late and very
unequally among men.

The master who used to teach me when I was
in one of the junior forms at school, and who,
without casting any reflection upon him, was neither

a Rollin nor a Lhomond, used to tell us to amuse ourselves during the holidays by reading Massillon's *Petit Carême*. That was because he wanted us to believe that he read it himself, and so make an impression upon us. A child that could take an interest in the *Petit Carême* would be nothing short of a monstrosity. Personally, I don't think such works as that attractive at any age.

When you are writing for children, do not assume a style for the occasion. Think your best and write your best. Let the whole thing live; let everything in your narrative be on a generous scale; let there be plenty of breadth and power. That is the one secret of pleasing your readers.

Having said that, I should have said all had it not been for the fact that, for ten years past, we French people—and, I verily believe, all the world besides—have been deluding ourselves with the idea that we only ought to let children read books about science, for fear of addling their brains with poetry.

So firmly is this belief implanted in people's minds, that nowadays when anyone brings out a new edition of Perrault, it is only intended for artists and bibliophiles. Look at Perrin's editions for example, or Lemerre's: they are bought solely by collectors, who have them bound in hand-tooled full morocco.

Then look at the illustrated catalogues of children's gift-books. Look at the sort of things that are displayed to tempt the children's eyes: crabs, spiders, caterpillars' nests, gas-engines. It's no encouragement to be a child. Every year we and our families are flooded out by books of popularised science as countless as the waves of the ocean. We are blinded—overwhelmed—by them. But, amid them all, nothing to please the eye, no noble thoughts, no art, no taste, nought of human nature: only chemical and physiological phenomena.

Yesterday, someone showed me *The Boy's Book of Industrial Marvels!* Another ten years, and we shall all be electricians!

Why, the worthy Monsieur Louis Figuier's usual placidity utterly deserts him at the mere idea of it still being possible for little French boys and girls to read about *Peau d'Ane.* He has written a preface for the special purpose of impressing on parents the importance of taking Perrault's tales away from their children, and of presenting them with the works of his friend Doctor Ludovicus Ficus instead. " Come! shut that book, please, Mademoiselle Jeanne: no more of the *Blue Bird* which you like so much that you shed tears over it. Come! look alive! and learn up all about the theory of etherisation. Here are you, seven years old, and no opinions on the anæsthetic properties of protoxide

of azote!" Monsieur Louis Figuier has found out
that fairies are creatures of the imagination, and
therefore he cannot bear that children should be
told anything about them. He talks to them about
guano: there is no imagination about that. But,
doctor, fairies exist precisely because they are
imaginary. They exist in those artless and un-
rivalled imaginations that are naturally receptive of
a form of poetry which never grows old—the poetry
of national tradition.

The most insignificant little book, if it inspires a
poetical idea, or suggests a noble sentiment; if, in a
word, it touches the soul, is more valuable to
children and young people than a wilderness of your
books about machinery.

We must have tales for little children, and tales
for big ones, tales that make us laugh or weep, that
waft us away to the realms of enchantment.

Only to-day I have received with the greatest
pleasure a book entitled *The World Bewitched*, containing about a dozen fairy tales.

The kindly and learned man who has gathered
them together remarks, in his preface, on the immemorial craving of the human soul for stories of
enchantment.

The need men have to forget the real world, with
its disappointments and mortifications, is a need that
is universal. It is the gift of imagination rather

than the gift of laughter that distinguishes man
from the lower animals, and sets the seal upon his
superiority.

A child feels it—this dream-hunger. He feels
his imagination stirring within him, and he craves
for fairy tales.

Refashioning the world in their own way, the
weavers of fairy tales prompt the weak, the simple,
and the young to refashion it in theirs. This is
why their influence is of the most sympathetic order.
They stir the imagination, they quicken the feelings,
they stimulate the affections.

Never fear that they will mislead the child by
filling his mind with useless notions about hob-
goblins and fairies. The child knows well enough
that such delightful apparitions are not of this
world. It is rather your popularised science that
does the mischief, that gives him false impressions
that are so difficult to eradicate. Little boys are
plentifully endowed with faith, and, when Monsieur
Verne tells them so, they will readily believe that
you can go up to the moon in a trajectile dis-
charged from a cannon, and that a body can defy
the laws of gravitation with impunity.

Such travesties of the ancient and venerable
science of astronomy have neither truth nor beauty
to recommend them.

What benefit can a child derive from slipshod

science, from so-called practical literature that appeals neither to the mind nor to the heart.

Rather must we turn again to the beautiful legends of the world, to the poetry of poets and peoples, to whatsoever thrills us with a sense of holiness and charm.

Unhappily, there are a great many chemists abroad just now who look on the imagination with mistrust. They are wrong! For she it is that sows the seeds of Beauty and Virtue up and down the world. She alone leads to greatness. Never, O ye mothers, never fear that she will injure your children. Rather will she hold them safe from vulgar faults and facile errors.

II

DIALOGUES UPON FAIRY TALES

LAURE. OCTAVE. RAYMOND

LAURE

THE purple belt that lay athwart the sunset has faded away; the horizon is bright with a glow of orange, and above it the sky is of the palest green in hue. See! There is the first star; see how white it shines, how tremulous it glows. And, look! another, and yet another! Soon they will be too numerous to count. The trees in the park have grown black, and they loom large and mysterious. That little path which leads down between that hedge of thorn, that little path whose every stone I know—how deep down, how adventurous, how mysterious it appears to-night. Whether I will or no, my imagination tells me that this path leads into the fairy realms of dreamland. How lovely is the night, how sweet it is to breathe. I am listening, cousin; talk to us of fairy tales, since you have so many curious things to relate

concerning them. But, I pray you, do not mar
them for me. Let me tell you at once that I adore
them, and it is herein that I feel a little vexed with
my daughter, who keeps wanting to know whether
"it's really true" about giants, ogres, and fairies.

RAYMOND

She is a child of the age, a sceptic before she
has cut her wisdom-teeth. I am not of that school.
I am no lover of philosophy in short frocks, and I
believe in fairies. Fairies exist, cousin, because
man made them. Whatever things we imagine,
these same things are real. They are the only
realities. If an old monk came to me and said,
"I have seen the Devil; he has two horns and a
tail," I should make reply to that same old monk,
and say, "Father, even supposing the Devil did
not exist already, you have created him. He exists
now without a shadow of a doubt. Take care he
doesn't have you." Cousin, mind you believe in
fairies, giants, and all the rest.

LAURE

Oh! Let's come to the fairies; never mind the
rest. You were saying just now that learned men
were occupying themselves with our fairy tales.
Well, then, I say again, I am terribly afraid they

will ruin them for me. Fancy taking little Red
Riding Hood out of the nursery to drag her to
the Institute. Oh! horror!

OCTAVE

I thought our present-day men of learning had
more disdain in their composition. But I see that
you are a good-natured set of fellows, that you
don't look down on stories that are the last word
in absurdity and puerility.

LAURE

Fairy tales are absurd and puerile if you like;
but I find it very difficult to grant; I love them so
much.

RAYMOND

Oh! grant it, cousin! grant it and never fear.
The *Iliad*, too, is a childish thing, and it is the
noblest poem that man can read. The purest poetry
is the poetry that was sung by nations in their
infancy. The races of the world are like the night-
ingale in the song: they sing well so long as their
hearts are light. As they grow old, they become
grave, learned, careworn, and then their finest poets
are but splendid rhetoricians. Certainly, "Sleeping
Beauty" is a childish thing, and that is why it

resembles a passage from the *Odyssey*. The beautiful simplicity, the divine ignorance of the primitive ages, for which we look in vain in the literary productions of classical eras, are preserved like a flower with all its perfume in the fairy tales and folk-songs of the world. Let us hasten to add, like Octave, that the tales are very irrational. If they were not absurd, they would not charm. You may rely upon it that the things people call irrational are the only things that are beautiful and sweet to the taste, the only things which lend grace to life and prevent us from dying of ennui. A sensible poem! A sensible statue! Why, everyone would be yawning at them, even your sensible men themselves. For, look you, cousin! Those flounces on that skirt of yours, those pleats and puffs and knots— how absurd the whole thing is, and how delicious. I tender you my congratulations.

LAURE

No more about fal-lals, please; you know nothing about them. I grant you that it does not do to be too uniformly sensible in art. But in life——

RAYMOND

The only beautiful things in life are the passions, and the passions are absurd. The finest of all has

the least of reason in it, and that is Love. There
is one that is somewhat less irrational than the rest,
its name is Avarice; but Avarice is appallingly
ugly. Dickens used to say that mad people were
the only ones that interested him. Woe to him
who does not now and then mistake a windmill for
a giant. The great-hearted Don Quixote was his
own enchanter. He measured everything by his
own great soul. That is not being made a dupe
of, mark you! Your real dupes are those who
never see aught of grandeur or loveliness in the
world.

OCTAVE

It appears to me, Raymond, that this "absurdity" which you value so highly has its origin
in the imagination, and that the idea to which
you have just given expression in such a brilliant
paradox simply amounts to this, that the imagination makes an artist of a sensitive man, and a hero
of a brave one.

RAYMOND

That is a pretty accurate description of one
aspect of my idea. But I should very much like
to know what you understand by the word "imagination"; and if, in your view, it is the faculty of

calling up to one's mind the things which are or the things which are not.

OCTAVE

My whole knowledge is limited to planting cabbages, and I should talk of imagination pretty much as a blind man would discourse on colours. But it is my belief that imagination is not worthy of the name save when it gives life to fresh forms or new ideas, save, that is to say, when it creates.

RAYMOND

Then imagination, according to your definition of it, is not a human faculty at all. Man is utterly incapable of imagining what he has never seen, or heard, or felt, or tasted. In this matter I am content to be old-fashioned; I swear by my old friend Condillac. All ideas come to us through the medium of the senses, and imagination consists not in the creation but in the piecing together of ideas.

LAURE

How can you say such things? Why! I can behold angels when I wish to!

R

RAYMOND

You see little boys and girls with goose wings. The Greeks used to see centaurs, sirens, and harpies, because they had previously seen men, horses, women, fishes, and birds. Now, take Swedenborg ; he possesses imagination. He tells us all about the inhabitants of Mars, Venus, and Saturn. Well, not a single attribute does he give them that is not to be found on this earth. But he combines them in the most violently extravagant manner. He raves all the time. Now see, on the other hand, what a beautiful, childlike imagination can produce. Homer—or, to speak more accurately, the unknown rhapsodist to whom we give that name— makes a young woman rise up from the grey sea " like unto a cloud." She speaks and she bemoans her fate, but with heavenly calm. " Alas ! Oh my child," says she, "wherefore did I nurture thee ? Hapless is the destiny for which I brought thee forth in my house. But I will go to the snowy summits of Olympus. I will enter the brazen house of Zeus. I will fold my arms about his knees, and I believe that he will grant my prayer." She speaks ! It is Thetis, a goddess ! Nature supplied the woman, the sea, and the cloud-drift ; the poet wove them together. Poetry and enchantment are all dependent on these happy associations of ideas. See, there, through the dark tracery of these interwoven branches, a moon-ray steals along the silvered boles of the birches. It trembles, and, lo! it is a ray no more; it is the white wing of a fairy. Children, if they saw it, would run away with a delicious terror in their breasts. Thus it was that the fairies and the gods came into being. In the supernatural world there is not so much as an atom that does not exist in the natural world.

LAURE

What a medley, to be sure, of Homer's goddesses and Perrault's fairies!

RAYMOND

Both are identical in origin and in nature. Your kings, your Prince Charmings, your fairy princesses lovely as the light of day, your giants—at once the terror and delight of little boys and girls —were gods and goddesses once upon a time, and filled our remote forefathers, the children of the race, with joy or terror. *Hop-'o-my-thumb* and *Blue Beard* are antique and venerable tales, which come to us from distant—very distant—lands.

LAURE

Now, where *do* they come from?

RAYMOND

Ah! did I but know! Some people have maintained, and would maintain to-day, that they hail
from the Hindu Koosh. They will have it that
they were invented beneath the terebinth trees of
that bleak and homeless region by the wandering
forefathers of the Greeks, the Latins, the Celts,
and the Germans. That is a theory that has
been held by very grave and learned men, who, if
they err at all, err not from flippancy. And one
needs a lively brain to construct scientific theories
at random. A polyglot may unaided flounder in a
score of languages. The wiseacres of whom I am
speaking never flounder in any circumstances. But
certain facts relating to the tales, the allegories,
and the legends, to which they would fain ascribe
an Indo-European origin, put them in a terrible
quandary. When they have taken prodigious pains
to prove to you that *Peau d'Ane* comes from the
Hindu Koosh, and that the tale of Reynard the
Fox is of exclusively Japhetic origin, behold!
an explorer arrives with the news that he has discovered Reynard among the Zulus, and that *Peau
d'Ane* is a household word among the Papuans.
This is a dreadful blow to their theory. But
theories are born to serve as targets, to be put out
of joint, to be distended, and finally to burst like

bubbles. However, one thing is likely enough, to wit, that fairy tales—particularly Perrault's—are derived from the oldest traditions of the human race.

OCTAVE

One moment, Raymond. I know little enough of present-day science, and I am much more of a farmer than a scholar; but I remember having read in a very well-written little book that the giants or ogres were none other than those Huns who ravaged Europe in the Dark Ages, and that the story of Blue Beard was based on the only too well authenticated story of that monster of iniquity—the Maréchal de Retz, who was hanged in the reign of Charles VII.

RAYMOND

We have done away with those ideas, my dear Octave, and the little book you mention, which was written by the Baron Walckenaer, is only so much waste paper. True, the Huns overran the face of Europe at the end of the eleventh century like a swarm of locusts, and appalling barbarians they were; but the form in which their name appears in the Romance languages conflicts with Baron Walckenaer's suggested derivation. Diez assigns a far more remote origin to the word "ogre." He

derives it from the Latin *orcus*, which, according to
Alfred Maury, is of Etruscan origin.   Orcus is the
God of Hell, the Devourer, who feeds on flesh,
preferably the flesh of new-born babes.   Now Gilles
de Retz was undoubtedly hanged at Nantes in 1440,
but not for having butchered his seven wives.   The
details of his story bear no resemblance to the fairy
tale, and it is doing Blue Beard an injustice to con-
found him with that abominable old villain.   Blue
Beard is not so black as he is painted.

LAURE

Not so black as he is painted ?

RAYMOND

He is not black at all, for he is nothing more nor
less than the sun

LAURE

What ! did the sun kill his wives, and was he
in turn killed by a dragoon and a musketeer ?
That won't do at all !   I know nothing of your
Huns or your Gilles de Retz ; but I must say I
agree with my husband that it is much more in
accordance with common sense to suppose that an
historical fact . . .

RAYMOND

Ah! cousin, there is nothing so fallacious as common sense. You are like all the rest of the world. If error appeared absurd to everybody, there would be an end to errors. All the erroneous conclusions that have ever been arrived at are the result of common sense; beware of it, cousin, for all the foolish and criminal deeds that were ever wrought were wrought in its name. So leave it alone, and come back to Blue Beard, who is the sun. The seven wives whom he slays are the seven dawns, for is it not true that every day in the week the sun rises and puts an end to the dawn? The star that is celebrated in the hymns of the Veda has, I confess, in its Gallic form, taken on something of the ferocious aspect of a feudal tyrant; but the tyrant has retained one attribute which proves his antique origin, and which enables us to recognise in this wicked baron a former solar divinity. The beard to which he owes his name—the beard of cerulean hue—at once establishes his identity with the Indra of the Hindu scriptures, the god of the firmament, the god of sunshine and rain and thunder, whose beard is azure.

LAURE

Now tell me, cousin, please, whether the two knights—one of whom was a dragoon, and the other a musketeer—were also Indian deities.

Raymond

Have you ever heard of the Açvini and the Dioscuri?

Laure

No, never!

Raymond

The Açvini among the Hindus, and the Dioscuri among the Greeks, represent the morning and evening twilight. Thus, in the Greek myth, it is Castor and Pollux who release Helen, the light of Dawn whom Theseus, the sun, had been holding in thrall. The dragoon and the musketeer of the story do no more nor less when they set free their sister, Madame Blue Beard.

Octave

I do not deny the ingenuity of these interpretations, but I believe that they are utterly baseless. You put me and my Huns to rout just now, so let me tell you, in turn, that there is nothing new in your theory, and that my late grandfather, who was well up in Dupuis, Volney, and Dulaure, believed the Zodiac to be at the bottom of every religious system. He used, worthy man, to declare—and my poor mother used to be terribly scandalised—that Jesus Christ was the sun, and His twelve apostles the twelve months of the year.

But do you know, most learned sir, how a witty man utterly routed Dupuis, Volney, Dulaure, my grandfather, and all? Applying a similar theory to Napoleon I., he demonstrated by its means that Napoleon had had no real existence, and that his whole story was a myth. The hero, who is born in an island, who is victorious in the east and west, who loses his power in the north during the winter, and disappears in the ocean, is, says the author—I don't remember his name—quite evidently the sun. His twelve marshals were the twelve signs of the Zodiac, and his four brothers the four seasons. I am greatly afraid, Raymond, that you are treating Blue Beard very much in the same way as this worthy individual treated the First Napoleon.

RAYMOND

The author you mention was, as you say, a witty man, and a man of learning. His name was Jean Baptiste Pérès. He died in 1840 at Agen, where he had followed the occupation of librarian. His curious little book, entitled *Comme quoi Napoléon n'a jamais existé*, was printed, if I am not mistaken, in the year 1817. It was undoubtedly a very ingenious skit on Dupuis' methods. But the theory, of whose application I have given you but a solitary and therefore an unconvincing example, reposes on a solid foundation of comparative grammar and mythology. The brothers Grimm have, as you know, collected the folk-stories of Germany. Their example has been followed in nearly every other country, and we now possess collections of the folk-lore of the Scandinavian, Danish, Flemish, Russian, English, Italian, and Zulu races. Reading these tales, so diverse in their origin, we note with astonishment that they are all, or nearly all, variations of a comparatively limited number of types. Here, perhaps, is a Scandinavian tale that seems as though it had been modelled on French traditions, which, in turn, may reproduce all the principal features of an Italian folk-story. Now, the idea that these resemblances are to be attributed to successive interchanges of ideas between the peoples concerned, cannot be entertained. It has therefore been assumed that such narratives belonged to the human family, as a whole, before its separation into its several parts, and that it was during their immemorial sojourn in their common home—the cradle of the race—that these fables and allegories presented themselves to their imagination. But, as no one has ever heard either of a region or a period when the Zulus, the Papuans, and the Hindus herded their flocks in common, we are forced to the conclusion that the early imaginings of the human mind are universally the same, that the same phenomena have produced the same impressions among all primitive people, and that men, who experience the pangs of hunger, of love, and of fear, who have the same sky overhead and the same earth beneath their feet, have all, in order to give expression to their ideas of Nature and Destiny, invented the same little dramas. Similarly, our nursery tales were originally merely a presentment of life and its surroundings, simple enough in style to satisfy the artistic cravings of the most unsophisticated of human beings; and this presentment probably followed the same broad outlines among the white, yellow, and black races alike. This admitted, I think we should do wisely to adhere to the Indo-European tradition, and to our ancestors of the Hindu Koosh, without troubling ourselves further concerning other human families.

Octave

I am following you with much interest; but are you not afraid of exposing so recondite a subject to some danger in thus making it the subject of a casual conversation?

Raymond

To tell you the truth, I am disposed to entertain fewer apprehensions for my subject from the accidents of an informal talk than from the logical

developments of a written essay. Don't take an
unfair advantage of this avowal, for I warn you
that I shall withdraw it the moment you show any
inclination to employ it to my disadvantage. From
this point onwards I am going to lay down the law.
I am going to give myself the pleasure of being
certain of what I say. So take warning! If I con-
tradict myself, as in all probability I shall, I shall
show an equal degree of affection for each of the
opposing threads of my argument so as to be quite
sure of not doing an injustice to the correct one.
Well, then, take heed! I am going to show myself
harsh, uncompromising, and, if I can manage it, a
fanatic.

LAURE

We shall have an opportunity of seeing how such
an attitude suits your style of countenance. But
what compels you to assume it?

RAYMOND

Experience! Experience tells me that scepticism,
however extensive, ceases when one begins to speak
or to act. For no sooner does one begin to speak,
than one dogmatises. A man is bound to take
sides. Well, at all events, I shall spare you the
" perhapses," the " if I may say so's," the " as it

were's," and all the dialectic frills and furbelows
that only a Renan can wear with elegance.

OCTAVE

Oh ! dogmatise to your heart's content. But do
introduce some sort of order into your exposition ;
and, for goodness' sake, tell us what your thesis is
now that you have got one.

RAYMOND

Everyone who is guided by sound judgment in
matters of general research has recognised that the
tales of the fairies have their origin in the myths
of Antiquity. Max Müller has told us that fairy
tales are the modern patois of mythology, and that
if they are to be made the subject of scientific study,
the first thing we have to do is to trace back every
modern story to an older legend, and every legend
to the original myth.

LAURE

Well, and have you performed this task ?

RAYMOND

Had I indeed carried out such a stupendous
undertaking, I should not have a hair left on my

head, nor should I have the pleasure of looking on
you now, unless it were to peer at you from beneath
a green shade through four pairs of spectacles. The
work has not been accomplished, but sufficient data
have been collected to permit every scholar to hold
with certainty that our fairy tales are not the mere
random offspring of the imagination, but that in a
number of cases they are most closely connected
with the very essence of ancient thought and ancient
modes of speech. The old, tottering, decrepit deities,
long since in their dotage, and thrust out from all
share in human affairs, still serve to amuse our little
boys and girls. Such is ever the lot of the " grand-
fer "; and what task more suitable to the old age
of the former lords of heaven and earth could
possibly be found? Fairy tales are great religious
poems, poems which the men of the race have
forgotten maybe, but which our grandmothers,
endowed with longer memories, have piously retained. Such poems have grown childish, but yet
how sweetly they fall from the gentle lips of yon
old grandam, who has put aside her spinning-wheel
to tell them to her son's little ones, as they sit
huddled around her on the floor beside the hearth.

The tribes of the white races are scattered over
the earth ; some have gone to dwell beneath translucent skies, by shining headlands, where the blue
sea breaks in music on the shore ; others have held

on their way into those mournful regions where
the mists bedim the fringes of the grey north sea,
where monstrous shapes—half seen, half guessed
at—hover, vague and shadowy, in the twilight.
Others have pitched their camps amid those lonely
steppes where their horses find scanty pasture.
Others have made their couch upon the frozen
snow, with a firmament of steel and diamonds above
them. Some have gone to cull the flowers of gold
from fields of granite ; and India's sons have drunk
of the rivers of Europe. But, all the world over,
in hut or in tent, or by the fire kindled in the plain,
she who was once a little girl, but has now become
a grandmother in her turn, tells over again to the
little ones of to-day the stories which had charmed
her as a child. And always the characters and the
adventures are the same, only the narrator—though
she knows it not—sheds upon her tales the hues
of the air she has breathed so long, and of the
earth which has nourished her, and which is soon
to gather her to its bosom again. And then once
more the tribe renew their wanderings, 'mid toil
and danger, leaving the old mother to sleep the
unawakening sleep amid the youthful and the aged
dead, while they fare ever farther and farther from
the sunrise. But the tales that have issued from
her lips—now cold in death—take flight like
Psyche's butterflies, and, lighting anew, fragile yet

immortal, on the lips of other grandams, glisten in the wondering eyes of the newest nurslings of the ancient race. Who was it, then, who introduced *Peau d'Ane* to the little boys and girls of France—" Sweet France " as the song has it ? " Old Mother Goose," reply the learned in country lore—old Mother Goose, whose spindle and tongue were never at rest. The scholars grew hot on the scent : they found that old Mother Goose was none other than that Queen Pédauque whom the master sculptors placed above the porch of the church of Sainte Marie at Nesles in the diocese of Troyes, over the porch of Sainte Benigne at Dijon, over those of Saint Pourçain in Auvergne and Saint Pierre at Nevers. They identify old Mother Goose with Queen Bertrade, wife and godmother to King Robert ; with Queen Berthe Bigfoot, the mother of Charlemagne ; with the Queen of Sheba, who, being an idolatress, had a cloven foot ; with the swan-footed Freya, the fairest of the Scandinavian goddesses ; with Sainte Lucie, whose body, like her name, was composed of Light. But this is hunting very far afield, and one may lose oneself in such a quest. For who and what is Mother Goose, but the mother of us all, the mother of our mothers, of the women of simple hearts and vigorous arms who wrought at their daily task with a grand humility, and who, when withered with age, when,

like the crickets, they had neither flesh nor blood,
still prattled by the chimney corner weaving those
long stories to all the bratlings of the family, stories
that would bring a world of visionary shapes before
their eyes. And the streams of mystic poetry,
the poetry of field and wood and fountain, flowed
fresh and virginal from the lips of the toothless
crone, even as the clear crystal flood which bubbles
forth spontaneously from a hidden spring. Upon
the ancestral canvas, upon the ancient Hindu background, Mother Goose embroidered the pictures
that she knew so well—the castle with its great
towers, the cottage, the fruitful field, the dim forest,
the beautiful ladies, the fairies so familiar to the
village-folk, fairies whom Joan of Arc might have
seen at eventide beneath the great chestnut by the
margin of the well . . .

Well, cousin, have I ruined your fairy tales for
you ?

LAURE

Go on, please ! Go on ! I am all attention.

RAYMOND

Had I to choose, I would with all my heart
sacrifice a whole library of philosophers rather than
part with *Peau d'Ane*. In the whole range of our

s

literature, none, save La Fontaine, has understood
like Mother Goose the poetry of the soil, the
strong and abiding charm of simple, homely
things.

But I must not omit to mention some important
considerations that are apt to be overlooked in the
course of a casual conversation. The primitive
languages were all pictorial, and they invested
everything with a living soul. The stars, the
clouds, "the kine of heaven," the daylight, the
winds, and the dawn—they endowed them all
with human feelings. From these picture-words,
words that lived and had a soul, sprang the myth,
and from the myth the fairy tale. The fairy tale
was incessantly undergoing changes, for change is
the essence of existence. The fairy tale was looked
on as being literally true, and, as good fortune
would have it, no clever people came along to
prate about allegories, and slay it at a stroke.
Good folk saw in *Peau d'Ane*, *Peau d'Ane* and
nothing more—nor less. Perrault sought for
nothing deeper in the story. Then came Science
and, at a glance, took in the long road the myth
and the tale had travelled, and Science said : "The
Dawn became *Peau d'Ane*." But Science should
add that, as soon as *Peau d'Ane* was thought of,
she took on a physiognomy, and enjoyed an individual existence of her own.

LAURE

I now begin to see the drift of what you are telling us. But you have mentioned *Peau d'Ane*, and I will confess to you that there is one thing in the story that revolts me beyond expression. Was it an Indian's idea that *Peau d'Ane's* father should conceive that odious passion for his daughter?

RAYMOND

Let us examine the real significance of the myth, and the incest at which you are so horrified will appear in quite an innocent light. *Peau d'Ane* is the Dawn; she is daughter to the Sun. When the king is described as being in love with his daughter, the meaning is that the Sun, when he rises, hastens after the Dawn. Similarly, in the Vedic mythology, Prajâpati, the Lord of Creation, the protector of every creature—who is identical with the Sun—pursues his daughter Uschas, the Dawn, who flees before him.

LAURE

Sun or no sun, your king revolts me, and I have a grudge against those who created him.

RAYMOND

They were innocent, and therefore immoral . . .
Nay, spare your protests, cousin; corruption is the
raison-d'être of morality, just as violence necessitates
the making of laws. This love which the king
entertains for his daughter, which is religiously
respected by tradition and by Perrault, bears witness
to the story's venerable antiquity. Incest was
looked on without horror in those families of
simple herdsmen, where the father was known as
"The one who protects," the brother as "The
one who aids," the sister as "The one who con-
soles," the daughter as "The one who herds the
cows," and the husband and wife as "The strong
ones." These neatherds of the Land of the Sun
had not invented Shame. In those days, the
woman, being devoid of mystery, was devoid of
danger. The patriarch's will alone decided whether
or not the aspiring bridegroom should bear away
his bride in the chariot drawn by two white oxen.
If, from the nature of the case, the union of a
father with his daughter was a rare occurrence,
such a union was not condemned. *Peau d'Ane's*
father did not create a scandal. Scandal is a pre-
rogative of highly civilised societies; it is, indeed
among their favourite distractions.

OCTAVE

Well, well! But I am convinced that your explanations are valueless. The moral sense is innate in mankind.

RAYMOND

Morality is merely custom reduced to a science. It varies with every country, and in none does it remain ten years the same. Yours, for instance, Octave, does not very closely resemble that of your father. The "innate" theory, moreover, is mere moonshine.

LAURE

Never mind about morality and innate ideas, please; they are highly tedious topics. Let us get back to *Peau a'Ane's* father, the Sun.

RAYMOND

You will remember that he nurtured in his stables, among horses of the noblest breed, richly caparisoned and stiff with gold and embroidered trappings, an ass—so the story runs—" of so strange a breed, that its litter, instead of being foul, was strewn every morning with splendid golden crowns and louis d'or of every description."

Now, this ass, onager, zebra, or whatever it may be, is the courser of the Sun, and the louis d'or with which it strews its litter are the discs of light which it scatters down through the interwoven branches. Its skin is emblematic of the gathering clouds. The Dawn shrouds herself therein, and disappears. You remember that charming scene where *Peau d'Ane*, in her sky-blue robe, is seen by the Beautiful Prince, who looks through the keyhole. This prince, the king's son, is a ray of sunlight . . .

LAURE

. . . Streaming through the door, that is to say between a rift in the clouds, I suppose.

RAYMOND

Most aptly stated, cousin ; and I see that you have quite a gift for comparative mythology. Now let us take the simplest story of them all, the story of the young girl who lets fall from her lips two roses, two pearls, and two diamonds. This young damsel is the dawn that causes the flowers to unfold their petals and bathes them with light and dew. Her wicked sister who vomits toads is the mist. Cinderella, besmutted with ashes, is the dawn obscured by clouds ; the young prince that weds her is the sun.

Octave

So, then, Blue Beard's wives are each of them the dawn; *Peau d'Ane* is the dawn; the damsel that lets fall roses and pearls is the dawn; Cinderella is the dawn. You give us nothing but dawns!

Raymond

Because the dawn, the magnificent Indian dawn, is the richest source of Aryan mythology. She is celebrated under a multiplicity of names and forms in the Vedic hymns. No sooner has night fallen, than men call upon her name and await her coming with a longing mingled with fear.

"The Dawn, beloved by us from of old, will she return? Will the powers of darkness be routed by the God of Light?" But she comes, the fair maiden. "She draweth nigh unto every house, and every man rejoiceth in his heart. 'Tis she, the daughter of Dyaus, the divine herdswoman who, every morning, drives afield the kine of heaven which, from their heavy udders, drop a fresh and quickening dew upon the parching earth."

As her coming was hailed with chants, so shall her flight be sung in a hymn to celebrate the triumph of the sun.

"Behold! here is yet another mighty deed that thou hast wrought, O Indra! Thou hast smitten the daughter of Dyaus, a woman hard to overcome. Yea! the daughter of Dyaus—the Glorious One, the Dawn — thou, O Indra, hast scattered her limbs asunder. The Dawn cast herself down in her shattered car, fearing lest Indra, the bull, should smite her. Her car lay there in fragments, but as for her she fled afar."

The primitive Hindu made himself various pictures of the dawn, but the picture was always instinct with life, and the pale and feeble reflections of it are still discernible in the stories which we have just mentioned, as well as in *Little Red Riding Hood*. The colour of the hood worn by the little maiden is an important indication of her celestial origin. The task of carrying cakes and butter to her grandmother enables us to connect her with the Dawn of the Vedas, who is a messenger. With regard to the wolf which eats her up . . .

LAURE

It is a cloud.

RAYMOND

Not so, cousin, it is the sun.

LAURE

The sun! A wolf?

RAYMOND

Yes, the devourer with the shining fur, Vrika, the Vedic wolf. Do not forget that two solar deities—the Lycian Apollo of the Greeks and the Apollo Soranus of the Latins—have the wolf for an emblem.

OCTAVE

But what connection is there between the sun and a wolf?

RAYMOND

When the sun dries up the water in the troughs, parches the meadows, and sears the hide of the starving oxen that gasp and pant with their tongues lolling from their mouths, does he not resemble a hungry wolf? The hide of the wolf is bright, and his eyes are ablaze; he shows his white teeth; his jaws and his loins are strong. The colour of his dazzling hair and eyes, and the destroying might of his jaws, prove that he is the sun. Here in this moist country, where the apple-trees bloom in abundance, you fear the sun but little, Octave; but Little Red Riding Hood has come from afar and traversed many a sun-scorched tract.

LAURE

The Dawn dies, and the Dawn is born again. But Little Red Riding Hood dies and comes back no more. It was wrong of her to stay gathering nuts and listening to the wolf; but is that a reason why she should be devoured without mercy? Were it not better that she should come forth again from the wolf's belly, as the Dawn issues from the darkness?

RAYMOND

Your pity, cousin, is very much to the point. Mother Goose had become rather hazy about the way the story ends, but at her age it is pardonable if one grows a trifle forgetful.

But the grandams of Germany and England know well enough that Little Red Riding Hood dies and comes to life again like the dawn. They tell how a huntsman opened the beast's belly and drew therefrom the rosy child, who gazed about her in wide-eyed amazement, saying, " Oh, what a fright I've had, and how dark it was in there!"

I was in your little girl's room just now looking at one of those coloured picture-books which Walter Crane, the Englishman, illuminates with such a wealth of fantasy and humour. He is possessed of an imagination which combines the qualities of homeliness and learning. He has the true feeling for what is legendary and a love for the realities of life: he reveres the past and enjoys the present. His is essentially the English outlook. The book I was

turning over contained the story of Little Red
Riding Hood (our *Petit Chaperon Rouge*). The
wolf devours her, but a gentleman-farmer in green
coat, yellow breeches, and top-boots puts a bullet
between its cruel glaring eyes, slits open its belly
with his hunting-knife and releases the child, who
comes forth fresh as a rose.

> " Some sportsman (he certainly was a dead shot)
>   Had aimed at the Wolf when she cried ;
> So Red Riding Hood got safe home, did she not,
>   And lived happily there till she died."

Such is the truth of the matter, cousin ; and you
guessed that it was so. Now Sleeping Beauty, whose
story is a piece of deep and simple poetry . . .

OCTAVE

She is the Dawn !

RAYMOND

Not so ! Sleeping Beauty, Puss in Boots, and
Hop o' my Thumb belong to another group of
Aryan legends : a group which symbolises the strife
between Winter and Summer, the perpetual renova-
tion of the natural world, the story, everlastingly
re-enacted, of the universal Adonis, that Rose of
the World that withers and blossoms anew eternally.
Sleeping Beauty is none other than Asteria, own
sister to Latona, and identical with Core and Perse-

phone. It was a happy inspiration of the popular
mind to choose as the symbol of light the earthly
form upon which light most lovingly lingers.
But give me Sleeping Beauty as she appears
in Virgil's story of Eurydice or in the Brun-
hilde of the Edda. The former was stung by a
snake, the latter was pricked by a thorn. The
Grecian maid was rescued from eternal darkness by
a poet and the Scandinavian by a warrior. It is
the ordinary fate of the lovely heroines of mythology to fall into a trance when scratched by anything that is sharp, be it thorn, talon, or spindle. In
a legend of the Deccan, discovered by Miss Frere, a
little girl pricks herself with a talon which a Rakchasa
had left in a doorway ; she swoons away immediately. A king passes by, kisses her and brings her
back to life again. The distinctive characteristic
of those stories of the strife between Summer and
Winter is that they never come to an end. Perrault's story begins again when it seemed to be
over and done with. Sleeping Beauty weds the
Prince, and from their union are born two children,
the lesser Day and the lesser Dawn, the Æthra
and Hemeros of Hesiod, or if you prefer it, Phœbus
and Artemis. In the Prince's absence, his mother,
an ogress, a Rakchasa, that is to say the Terror of
Night, threatens to devour the two royal children,
who are only saved by the timely return of Kin

Sun. In the west of France, Sleeping Beauty has a rustic sister whose story is related with much naïveté in a very ancient song. This song tells how a little girl named Guenillon was sent into the woods by her father to gather nuts, how she found the branches beyond her reach, and how she pricked her finger with a thorn and fell into a deep slumber. Then, so the story runs, three gallant knights came riding by. "I spy a maiden," cried the first. "She is asleep," cried the second. "She shall be my lady-love," said the third, and laughed a rollicking laugh.[1]

---

[1] "Quand j'étais chez mon père,
Guenillon,
Petite jeune fille,
Il m' envoyait au bois,
Guenillon.

Pour cueillir la nouzille,
Ah ! Ah ! Ah ! Ah ! Ah !
Guenillon,
Saute en guenille.

Il m' envoyait au bois
Pour cueillir la nouzille !
Le bois était trop haut,
La belle trop petite . . .

Le bois était trop haut,
La belle trop petite—
Elle se mit en main
Une tant verte épine.

Elle se mit en main
Une tant verte épine
A la douleur du doigt
La bell' s'est endormie . . .

There the legend has fallen into the last stages
of corruption, and it would be impossible, in the
absence of other evidence, to recognise, in the
rustic Guenillon, the heavenly light which languishes
during the winter and regains his strength in the
springtide.

The Persian Epic, the *Schahnameh*, introduces
us to a hero whose fate resembles that of Sleeping
Beauty. Isfendiar, whom no sword could wound,
was destined to die of a thorn which pierced his eye.
The story of Balder in the Scandinavian Edda
presents a still more striking resemblance to Sleeping Beauty.

Just as the fairies gathered round the cradle of

> A la douleur du doigt
> La bell' s'est endormie,
> Et au chemin passa
> Trois cavaliers bons drilles.
>
> Et le premier des trois
> Dit : " Je vois une fille."
> Et le second des trois
> Dit " Elle est endormie,"
> Et le second des trois,
>   Guenillon,
>
> Dit: " Elle est endormie."
> Dit le dernier des trois,
>   Guenillon,
>
> Dit : " Ell' sera ma mie,"
>   Ah ! Ah ! Ah ! Ah ! Ah !
>   Guenillon,
>   Saute en guenille. . . ."

the king's daughter, so all the gods come to look upon Balder, the divine infant, and swear that no harm shall come to him from anything on earth; but the mistletoe which grows not upon the ground was forgotten by all the immortals, just as the king and queen forgot the old hag who was turning her spinning-wheel away up in one of the towers of their castle. A spindle pricks the beautiful princess; a branch of mistletoe is the death of Balder.

> " So on the floor lay Balder dead ; and round
> Lay thickly strewn swords, axes, darts, and spears,
> Which all the Gods in sport had idly thrown
> At Balder, whom no weapon pierced or clove ;
> But in his breast stood fixt the fatal bough
> Of mistletoe, which Lok the Accuser gave
> To Hoder, and unwitting Hoder threw." [1]

LAURE

All that is very beautiful ; but have you nothing to tell us about the little dog Puff that lay asleep on the Princess's bed. She seems to me a dainty little animal. Puff was fondled on the lap of many a marquise, and I can picture Madame de Sévigné caressing her with the hands that penned those graceful letters of hers.

---

[1] M. Arnold : *Balder Dead.*

RAYMOND

Well then, to please you, we will see to it that
Mademoiselle Puff has a celestial ancestry. We
will trace her descent back to Saramâ, the female
dog that pursues the Dawn, or to the hound Seirios,
the guardian of the stars. That, I trow, is a pedi-
gree worth having! Puff has now only to prove
her quarterings to be made Canoness of the Chapter
of a canine Remiremont. But it would need the
authority of a four-footed D'Hozier to establish so
complicated a genealogical claim. I shall limit
myself to pointing out one ramification of her tree,
namely, the Finnish branch represented by the little
dog Flô, whose mistress addresses him thrice, saying :

" Go, my little dog Flô, and see if it will soon
be daylight."

When she had said this a third time, the day
broke.

OCTAVE

I really like the way you find places in heaven
for all the men and women and animals in these
tales of yours. Never was Roman emperor more
promptly assigned a dwelling-place among the con-
stellations. Now according to you, the Marquis
de Carabas cannot be anything less of a personage
than the sun himself.

RAYMOND

Not a doubt of it, Octave! This needy, humble individual who grows in wealth and power as time goes on, is the sun which rises in a mist and then shines forth in splendour in the clear air of noonday. Observe this point: the Marquis de Carabas comes forth from the water and arrays himself in brilliant apparel. What could be more obviously symbolical of the sunrise?

LAURE

But according to the story, the Marquis is a sluggish creature who is led by the nose. It is the cat who does all the acting and thinking, and it is only right that, like Puff, this cat should have a place in the heavens.

RAYMOND

And a place in the heavens he has; like his master, he represents the sun.

LAURE

I am very glad to hear it. But are his title-deeds in order, like Puff's? Can he prove his lineage?

RAYMOND

As Racine says:

" L'hymen n'est pas toujours entouré de flambeaux." [1]

Perhaps Puss in Boots is a descendant of the cats

---

[1] Hymen is not always surrounded by torches.

T

that drew the chariot of Freya, the Scandinavian
Venus, albeit the chroniclers of the tiles make no
mention of it.   There is one very ancient solar cat,
the Egyptian cat, identical with Ra, who recites a
part in a funeral service which has been translated
by Monsieur de Rougé.   " I am the Great Cat,"
says the animal, " who was in the avenue of the
tree of life, in An, on the night of the great com-
bat."   But this cat is a Cushite and a son of Shem
Puss in Boots is of the tribe of Japhet, and I cannot
see for the life of me how to establish any connection between them.

LAURE

This Great Cushite Cat who discourses so cryptic-
ally in that funeral service of yours, did he wear
boots and carry a wallet?

RAYMOND

There is no mention of it in the service.   The
boots of the Marquis's cat are analogous to the
Seven League Boots which Hop o' my Thumb puts
on, and which are symbolical of the swiftness of
light.   According to the learned Monsieur Gaston
Paris, Hop o' my Thumb was originally one of those
Aryan cattle-robbing deities who herded and stole
the oxen of heaven, a divinity after the style of the
infant Hermes, who is represented on vases cradled

in a shoe. The popular imagination assigned Hop o' my Thumb an abode in the smallest star of the Great-Bear group. By-the-by, you know that Jacquemart, who gave the world such beautiful etchings, had a fine collection of footgear. If one followed his example and made a museum of mythological shoes and so forth, one could fill up more than one glass case. Alongside of the Seven League Boots, the shoe of the infant Hermes, and the boots of the famous Puss, you would have to range the talaria worn by the adult Hermes, the sandals of Perseus, Cinderella's glass slipper, and the tight shoes of Marie, the little Russian girl. All these various coverings for the feet are expressive, each in its own way, of the swiftness of light and the courses of the stars.

LAURE

It was a mistake, was it not, when people said that Cinderella's slippers were made of glass?[1] It is impossible to imagine anything to put on one's feet being made of the same material as a decanter, for example. Slippers made of squirrel's skin[2] would be much more conceivable, though they would be hardly the things for a little girl to go to a ball in. To keep up the dance with such hot things on her feet as that she must have been dance-mad; but then

[1] Verre.   [2] Vair.

all young girls are dance-mad. They would foot it if their shoes were soled with lead.

RAYMOND

Cousin, I had warned you to beware of common-sense conclusions. Cinderella's slippers were not made of fur but of glass, glass as transparent as any that ever came from Saint Gobain, as transparent as spring water or rock crystal. You see, they were fairy slippers, and that does away with all your difficulties. A pumpkin becomes a coach; well, it was a fairy pumpkin, and what more natural than for a fairy pumpkin to become a fairy coach? The surprising thing would be if it did not. The Russian Cinderella has a sister who cuts off her big toe in order to get the slipper on, and the slipper becomes covered with blood. So the Prince learns to what an heroic subterfuge ambition had driven the girl.

LAURE

Perrault merely says that the two wicked sisters did their very utmost to squeeze their feet into the slipper, but that all their efforts were in vain. I like that better.

RAYMOND

That is also Mother Goose's account of the
matter. But if you had Sclavonic blood in your
veins you would be a little bloodthirsty, and the
lopped-off toe would be just to your taste.

OCTAVE

Raymond has been telling us a good deal about
fairy tales, but not a word has he said up to the
present about fairies themselves.

LAURE

True. But would it not be better not to dispel
their mystery, better to leave them vague and
undefined?

RAYMOND

You are afraid that these capricious creatures,
who can be good or wicked, young or old, as
their fancy takes them, who have such power over
Nature yet seem always on tiptoe to run and hide
themselves in her bosom—you fear that they would
resent our prying ways and slip through our fingers
just as we thought to seize them. They are made
of the moonbeam. Only the rustling of the leaves
tells you of their passing, and their voices mingle

with the murmur of the streams. Catch at their
golden raiment as they hurry by and you find but
a few dry leaves in your hand. I should never be
so impious as to chase them, but their name alone
suffices to reveal the secret of their nature.

The French word *fée* is the same as the
Italian *fata*, the Spanish *hada*, and the Portuguese
jada. In Provence they talk about *fade*, while in the
Berri country which George Sand made so famous
the word appears as *fadette*. All alike come from
the Latin *fatum*, which means Destiny. The fairies
have their origin in what is at once the gentlest and
the most tragic, the most intimate and most universal conception of the life of man. It is well that
a woman should typify Fate; for woman, like Fate,
is wayward, seductive, deceiving, a thing of charm,
unrest, and peril. It is perfectly true that a fairy
is godmother to every one of us, and that, as she
leans over our cradle, she dispenses gifts fraught
with bliss or bale, that remain with us to the end
of our days. Take any group of people; ask them
what they are, what has made them so, and what
they do. You will find that the ruling influence of
their destiny, be it happy or be it disastrous, is a
fairy. We all like Claude, because he sings so
well. He sings well because his vocal chords are
disposed to harmony. But who placed them thus
in Claude's throat? Why, a fairy! Wherefore did

the king's daughter prick herself with the old
crone's spindle? Because she was full of life and
just the least bit thoughtless. And who was responsible for that? The fairies!

This is just exactly what the fairy tales say, and
all the stores of human wisdom can no farther go.
For how is it, cousin, that you are witty, fair, and
kind? Because one fairy gave you kindness, another
a clever brain, and another a beautiful face. It
was done even as they commanded. A mysterious
godmother pre-ordains, at our birth, what all our
actions, all our thoughts shall be through life, and
we shall be just as good and enjoy just that measure
of happiness that she has meted out to us. Freedom
is a dream, the fairy is a reality. My friends, virtue,
like vice, is a necessity we cannot evade. Nay, I
know what you would say! But virtue is none the
less beautiful because it is involuntary, none the less
worthy of our adoration.

What takes us in an act of kindness is not the
price it costs but the good it works. Beautiful
thoughts are but emanations from beautiful souls
shedding around them their own substance, as per-
fumes are particles of flowers that melt upon the
air. The breath of a noble soul can be but noble
ever, even as the rose can smell but of the rose.
'Tis the will of the fairies. Cousin, you must
thank them.

LAURE

Enough, I will hear no more. Your wisdom is uncanny. I know the power the fairies have. I know their changeful moods. They have visited me with sinkings of the heart, with vexations and weariness, no less than other folk. But I know that above the fairies, above the wavering chances of the world, there soars that Everlasting Mind that has inspired our hearts with Faith, and Hope, and Charity. Cousin, good-night!

THE END

www.ingramcontent.com/pod-product-compliance
Lightning Source LLC
Chambersburg PA
CBHW022116080426

42734CB00006B/152